"I finished *Hopey* in one sitting tonight. It's a harrowing, inspiring journey of endurance filled with people you grow to care about deeply. This is not a novel filled with stock characters in familiar situations. The people that surround Hope are deeply flawed, sometimes horrifying, and often passionate on both sides of decency, colliding into the sheer life force that is Hope. Her story is a tribute to courage and acceptance and how experience decorates our lives in colors both bright & dark. It's how she wears them that leaves us changed."

—**George Fiscus**, Owner/Managing Partner, F&M Merchant Group

"Wow. Intense. Emotional. Poignant. I feel blessed to have had this pre-read. Hope has an amazing gift for storytelling. Lots of highlights stand out. I think the college entry exam story got to me the most, as well as the pacts she makes with her daughters and mother."

—**Harry Jeffreys**, VP, Global Quality Systems and Compliance, Bausch Health Companies Inc.

"I finished the book in one night!! I WANT MORE OMG! It is an amazing read. I loved it. It really brought me back to my childhood. So amazing! I was reading between baseball innings at a game, and I could not stop until it was finished!"

—**Jody Haas**, Owner/Operator, Shangri-Lon Salon

"Hope is amazingly perceptive about people and has that rare descriptive gift that marks the best writers. Hope captures the people in her life and makes them come alive on the page. The book is so compelling, I did not want to stop reading. There is more to tell, and I cannot wait to see what comes next. Hope is an excellent observer of human character, as well as being honest and outspoken about herself, without ever being whiney. In fact, she is immensely likable and relatable, even if the story is so unlike anything most people experience. The reader is with this author 100 percent, invested in the story and rooting for Hope's success."

—**Justin Robertson**, Researcher and Educational Consultant

"Page turner! From the very first page, I had trouble putting it down and would stay up way too late reading it. The writing, content, and storytelling style is captivating. I liked the snapshot and flash forward devices for transcending time and giving a nod to past experiences linking to current. I appreciate and like best the raw honesty and self-reflection throughout the piece. I admire the author's ability to unflinchingly capture deeply painful and difficult moments with a very matter-of-fact style. The book reflects how humans are able to transcend upbringing and trauma, how we are able to take life lessons, learn from chaos, be given second chances, believe in ourselves, be helped by mentors, and to create a totally different life for ourselves and our children—and, most importantly, to keep love, acceptance, and exploration at our core."

—**Jennifer Hottell**, Community Engagement Director, United Way of Monroe County

"I LOVE this book. I spent many nights staying up too late to finish it. The framework of alternating time frames really works, and it's important for the reader to have a reprieve from the intensity of the past. Holy cow. What a life this young lady has had."

—**Jane Banning**, Yoga and Fitness Instructor

"I did not stop reading it until I read the last word. It was so honest and brave. I grieved for what the little girl endured, and I cheered for her as she fought to find her way. I admired and celebrated with her as she moved into a 7,000 square foot house with or without 'window treatments' and as she climbed the professional ladder with tamed Janis Joplin hair. Such a story of courage, unconditional love, and insight. The book is a testimony of extraordinary resilience, courage, and ultimately the power of hope. An amazing read! Bravo!"

—**Audra Coleman**, Author, Artist, and Professor

"The book exemplifies this author's ability to put the reader in her shoes, what was normal for her as a child and early teen. Reading the early years made me want to go back and save her. Those times came together to shape her and turn her life into something amazing and inspirational. There is so much left unwritten. I only hope that she will continue this journey with her readers."

—**Susan Chambers**, Housing and Office Manager, Area 10 Agency on Aging

"A riveting story that is both inspiring and unbelievable, but one thing is for certain: You will be rooting for *Hopey* all the way to the corner office."

—**Melanie Neil**, VP of Commercial Operations, Stryker

"I found myself unable to take my eyes off the pages. I read the piece in its entirety in one sitting. This work is heart wrenching and all the while inspiring. I was transported to Hope's childhood and adolescence. It felt as if I were watching firsthand her trials and tribulations. I cannot wait to see what comes next."

—**Taylor Dukes**, Employee Benefits,
OneAmerica Financial Partners

"Hope is an inspirational and courageous author. Her insight and perspective are powerful and motivating. I highly recommend this book!"

—**Patty Klingbiel**, President and Principal,
The Connell Group

"*Hopey* is a must read, an inspiration to anyone going through tough times. She went through so much as a child and could have chosen an easier path. But she held strong and determined she would have more, do more, and here she is . . . amazing isn't enough!"

—**Kristie White-Scott**, Supernova

"A description of a life in development, in danger, in constant motion. Ms. Mueller aptly describes a child and young woman whose tumultuous upbringing has the reader thinking, 'I cant believe that happened to her,' and then, just as quickly, 'The same thing happened to me!' A poignant, fascinating, infuriating, and funny read about a hippie kid making her way under her own steam."

—**Meredith Merson**, Site Head of Quality,
Cardinal Health

"Loved *Hopey*! A reminder that you never completely know someone's story. Hope writes from her heart and shares stories of her unconventional upbringing and how her resilience helped shape the amazing person she is today. Looking forward to the second book."

—**Katy Dukes**, Rockstar Mom

"An emotional journey of growth and intellectual perseverance—resulting in this powerful story of insurmountable obstacles and the triumph of the human spirit. With no promises of acceptance or success, Mueller shares her bare bones experience to relate to the reader that NO MATTER what anyone must overcome, drive and love of life are the essential tools to achieve your goals."

—**Katy Zabriskie**, Partner, Zabriskie Enterprises

"To laugh, cry, feel anger, and such joy—all within a single short read. Great work by Hope Mueller, one of the most inspirational people I've ever met in my life. Her work is as beautiful and REAL as her heart."

—**Melissa Alberts**, Senior Director, Quality, Horizon Therapeutics

"*Hopey: From Commune to Corner Office* makes you look back at your life and wonder what it would be like if you reacted differently to tragedies and trials, allowing those to give you encouragement to chase your dream. It also offers hope that no matter what tribulations we face, we can choose our fate. The writing is mesmerizing and leaves you wanting more."

—**Jennifer Harp**, Elementary School Teacher

"The book is a testament of perseverance, acceptance, independence, and strength. It's about family ties and complex dynamics. It's about opening up and trusting people. It's about so much more that you read between the lines. I highly recommend it!"

—**Sasha Korobko**, Tech Lead and Women Empowerment and Education Leader, Rocketmiles

"I am amazed by the honesty of Hope's book, the tone in which it was written, and the fact that I read it in one sitting! You won't be able to put this down."

—**Carrie Buchwald**, Senior VP, Lake Forest Center for Leadership, Lake Forest Graduate School of Management

"I could not stop reading Hope's story. Poignant, brilliant, marvelous storytelling. Looking forward to her next book already!"

—**Debbie Ryan**, Lover of Stories

"*Hopey: From Commune to Corner Office* is a thoughtfully written true story that keeps you intrigued from the first sentence to the last. An amazing testament to the power of determination, hard work, and perseverance. Looking forward to additional work from this talented author!"

—**Alison Brown**, Corporate Compliance Officer, Romark L.C.

"As a fellow college town commune kid from the '70s, I can attest to the visceral accuracy the author portrays as she tells her story. A time of loose morals and questionable boundaries led many of us into personal dilemmas and hardships that were beyond our years and wisdom. The author shows this world through her unique viewpoints while honoring those with whom she shared her journey. The book is engaging and left me with a sense of relief and appreciation for the spark and strength of the human spirit. Worth a read."

—**Christian Brackett**, Community Paramedic/MIHP, Mission Health

"Reading about Hope's childhood was at times fascinating, other times distressing, and occasionally flat-out infuriating. The things she went through would have crushed many other people's spirits. But Hope is nothing if not a fighter. Through the adversity (not despite it), she hones her natural strengths and gains valuable insights, which help her become the professional powerhouse she is today. This book is a master class in the power of gratitude and positivity."

—**Jennifer Bushey**, Technical Specialist,
Meridian BioGroup

"Every one of us has had a childhood that provided memorable experiences, molded us through critical life lessons, and helped make us into the person we are as an adult. It is entirely within our freedom to choose the attitude and meaning we assign these experiences in order to make sense of our identity and tell our life story. Throughout this book, Hope Mueller's narration of her childhood and early adolescence is a stunning example of the power of gratitude, forgiveness, and appreciation, and the magnificence of the human spirit to defy falling prey to any less interpretation of whatever life serves up to us."

—**Dr. Alise Cortez**, Purpose/Engagement Catalyst
and Organizational Logotherapist

"Moments are many throughout life—those few we've shared up until now have shaped the future of what is to come."

—**Brad Mueller**, President,
Healthsmart International

hopey

hopey

From Commune to Corner Office

hope mueller

B *inspire*books

Published by Inspire Books
www.inspire-books.com

Cover Photography by Barbara Brennan
Cover Design by Dylan Wickstrom

ISBN: 978-1-950685-04-2 paperback
ISBN: 978-1-950685-05-9 hardcover
ISBN: 978-1-950685-06-6 ebook

Library of Congress: 2019905455

Printed in the United States

CONTENTS

DEDICATION

To my husband, Brad, this book would not be possible without you. To my daughters, Ashlei, Olivia, Brooke, and Lauren, thank you for making a pact with me before you were born. To my sister, Lori, thank you for the memories. Mom, thank you for our partnership in this lifetime.

PREFACE

The material in this book is the truth, as I know it, as I saw it, and experienced it through my eyes. I know now as a parent that my perception of the truth is wildly different than my children's. Therefore, I recognize that the other people's memories of the events described are different than my own. Everyone in this book is a lovely and decent human. The book was not intended to harm anyone, hurt anyone's feelings, or portray them negatively. Everyone involved in the publication, marketing and support of this book all confirm there is no intention of harm, hurt or disparagement.

I have changed names, made tweaks to settings and descriptions, to allow people to remain anonymous. There are two instances where I compressed time to support the flow and telling of the story. To the best of my ability I have remained honest to my perception of the truth.

Every childhood shapes a child. Mine was tumultuous, but here I am, standing strong and grateful. For that, I thank my mom, dad, husband, and all the people who helped me along the way.

I am now an executive, wife, and mother. I am blessed beyond measure to have a true partner in this life. My husband and I are raising our children, driving our careers, and loving each other unconditionally. He has accepted me for who I am, who I was, and he knows me.

hopey

THE OIL LAMP

2:00 a.m. There it is. The sounds.

The lurching, urging sounds coming from Mom's room. Again.

Frantic groans, oaths of intimacy, and the thumping of the headboard against the wall.

Lori slams open my bedroom door and commands, "Get up!"

I sit up and blink at her.

"We are not going to tolerate this anymore." The hate gleams in her eyes. "Not again. Not tonight. Today is the last day we are going to wake up to this."

My sister's barging in did not scare or wake me. The fucking noises had already done that. The sounds were ordinary middle-of-the-night passion that screamed me awake with the understanding that a strange man was in the house. Each time, fear and disgust formed in my mind with the knowledge of what was occurring.

I mostly hide from the noise, fold under my blankets and bury my head in my pillow, and plea for the sounds to stop. *Just stop. Just get done. Please cum and get it over with.*

Lori has other plans. This was it. Lori is going to put a stop to it. Her teenage wrath burns in her chest; the contempt contorts her face. She orders me again: "Get up!"

My sister's rage was as common as our mother's boozy sex escapades. I rub my eyes and push back my mass of unruly hair. I curl my hands into my lap and pat the spot next to me and ask her to sit.

"Just sit for a second, Lori." I pause. "Tell me, what can we really do?"

"Let's go in there and tell her to stop!"

I hesitate. I had already seen that scene, and it was imprinted on my mind. The twisted bodies and the soft groping still haunt me. It is not something I want to see again, at least not by choice.

Lori seethes. "I can't take it! And I'm not having you continue to go through this."

Her adrenaline is contagious. I agree and start to allow myself to relish the anger, nurse it.

It is true that I never want to wake up to this again. I shift out of bed, pull down my T-shirt, and pass my hand across my face. I take a steeling breath and gird myself for the next few hours of anger.

We march through the dank living room. Lori charges through the threadbare curtain that marks the divide into Mom's room. I fast tiptoe behind, in the eddy of her wake.

"No more! Get up!" She bellows. "We are not going to listen to you fucking all night." She glares at the fat, swarthy man entwined with mom and screams, "Get out!"

Surprise, embarrassment, and confusion flash across his face.

I am in awe. Lori's indignation is so pure. A wild beauty exudes from her fearlessness. I see, we all see, that Lori is at the height of her anger.

"Get out of my room!" Mom replies in a strangled cry.

I realize I am holding my breath; I exhale and pull on Lori's arm, not wanting to get into a fight with na-ked people. And I did not want to continue to look at

3

the man hovering over mom. I drag Lori to the kitchen and leave the lovers to unwind.

It is always the kitchen, the proverbial hearth. As humans, our evolutionary minds automatically lead us to the place of food and warmth when danger is looming. A sense of safety is found in a kitchen.

We wait. I stare at the floor. The floor is hardwood painted light blue. I wonder why somebody would paint a beautiful hardwood floor. The blue paint is shredded. Every effort to clean it is unsuccessful with the dark brown peeking through the light blue in scarring scratches. Grimy press-board cabinets with broken and missing hinges hang forlorn and seem to wait with us in the gathering storm.

Lori paces. I sit at our ancient wooden table and inspect the delicate oil lamp that rests in the center. The glass lamp is three feet tall, out of place in its elegance, like a foreign word in an English sentence. Red oil languishes heavy in the well of the lamp, and the chimney looks ready to break with its height and fragility.

I breathe. I wait. I had been here before. I had seen the culmination of emotion well up, and I knew it was unlikely that the night would pass without violence. My role as peacekeeper would be critical.

Interrupted coitus remained just that, interrupted. Mom and the man decide to join us in the kitchen, belly up to the table and settle into an edgy silence. The smarmy man, a bartender at Mom's work, didn't know the frenzied den he was entering, the culmination of years of fear and disturbed sleep. Instead of slinking out of the house, pulling on his greasy pants and quietly exiting, he was going to face the angry daughters.

I had fully expected Mom to enter the kitchen alone and ashamed in the guilty-milky way of the alcohol. Did she persuade him in joining this discussion? Did she plead for his assistance? What was she thinking? What was he thinking?

The embarrassed pair start with their cigarettes. It is a safe play, other than the introduction of a flame. The calming effect of the cigarette on the smokers begins, followed by a false sense of confidence.

I watch his thick fingers remove the cigarette, turn it, roll it between his finger and thumb, then the flick of the lighter. This ritual, this process, is savored and creates an instant solidarity among the couple and pauses time. I watch and wait for the nicotine smoke to choke out the smell of sex. The moment passes and Lori senses weakness. She comes alive with rage.

"Who the fuck are you?" Lori glowers at the man. "You are not part of this family. You need to get out of this house. This is not about you."

He is a grown man but no match for the years of dysfunction present at the sad table.

"I, uh, I was a counselor and I'm going to talk you guys through this," he said.

It is inconceivable, even to me, that this man thought he could help us, to assume that he had any answers or solutions. Even if he could help, was he, or Mom, in any condition to really discuss things intelligently? They came home hammered and looking to fuck, not have a deep discussion with teenage girls. His attitude fanned the flames of hatred, and Lori explodes.

She stands up shoving the table with her hips. The oil in the lamp sloshes. The flame menaces.

Lori's table thrust forces him out of his rickety seat. The man raises to his feet. He sends a plaintive glance at our mother. How far was he willing to go here? Clearly this is deep-seated family shit and, really, what could he do? He just wanted some drunken pussy with the waitress. She had bedded most of the men at the bar; it was just his turn, right? Why take on this fight?

He didn't. With a shrug and raised eyebrows, he walks out to Mom's mewling apology.

A sneer replaces Mom's pleading frown. How had her fun been spoiled by these girls? Fueled by the same anger that she had bestowed in the chests of her daughters, Mom's ability to turn from victim to incensed lover is quick.

"Who do you think you are?" she screeches. "You do not get to tell me what to do!"

Her indignant flare is no match for Lori. As the temporary peacemaker had departed, I have to reassume my role, but there is too much anger here. They both are yelling over each other. Their faces are red and fingers are pointed. The table groans under the pressure.

No breath. The chairs scrape new scars on the blue painted floor. No pause. The volume and intensity grows. The screaming is blinded fury.

We had been here before, the three of us. The anger is as palpable as the sticky grime on the refrigerator door. It is all too much. We have to push through it. The rage has to be engaged. There is too much adrenaline to pull back now, we have to move through. Some violence, some physical act, must occur in order to move on. The healing cannot begin until the enflamed hatred is made visible.

The best hope is an act of destruction of property. Property can be repaired or replaced. Attempting to avert violence on bodies is now the goal. Once the materials are crushed, the healing and the apologies could begin, but if a body is harmed, deeper scars would be born.

Lori grips the edges of the table and heaves it upward. As she flips the table, Mom and I scatter back. The lamp is sacrificed. It crashes spectacularly. The frail glass shatters. The red oil spreads heavy across the blue flecked floor.

We all stare with a collective breath. Had the wick been blunted with the sloshing from the first push of the table? Or would the clear blue flames race atop the spreading oil and catch fire to us all?

NIGHT CARE

I was speaking at a conference in Amsterdam. A few of the other speakers and I skipped the afternoon sessions to explore the canals and the city. The afternoon was bright and chilly as we turned the corner into the infamous red-light district. Passing a coffee house, a dense cloud of smoke rolled out into the crowd of tourists on the sidewalk. That smell enveloped me and invaded my brain and all my senses. Instantly I was transported back to my childhood.

What do other childhoods smell like? Downy? Dial soap? The sawdust cleaner that the janitor throws around at school when someone pukes? Mine is found in the single scent of the burning marijuana plant.

I was raised by my mother, a hippie, in the truest

sense of the word. She was not the current trust fund wannabe hippies of today; she was the real thing. Mom was a legitimate flowers-in-the-hair, Janis-Joplin-singing, Woodstock-attending, reeking-of-patchouli hippie. She was turned on, tuned in, and dropped out.

The first thing that struck people about Paula, my mom, was her cool confidence and easy sexuality. Lean, curvy, with the perfect evolutionary desired breast-waist-hip ratio, she moved her body forward naturally, leaning into men, and also drawing women toward her. Everyone loved her; she was magnetic. Relaxed with her body, she proffered light touches on arms for acquaintances and full body hugs for others. She wore little to no makeup and had long, dark hair that hung straight and heavy around a wide face with a straight-forward smile. Mom was not the typical Barbie doll beauty, but her allure was evident and she was never short on suitors.

Mom could strike up a conversation with anyone, and she ignored most social norms and expected behaviors. Strangers seemed comfortable around her, spilling their life stories in an elevator or waiting room. Perhaps because she was so comfortable with herself, others felt comfortable with themselves when around her. She had low tolerance for drama and did not participate in gossip. Mom never seemed nervous, anxious, or scared. Always relaxed and fully present, she engaged people with her eyes and held them there with her intellect. She was quick with an opinion, but open to other ideas, allowing for everyone to have ample space and presence for their own purposes.

That all sounds lovely, but in most ways, she was opposite of the idea of the "normal" mom. She didn't stay at home, cleaning was low on her priority list, and she cussed (a lot). She also drank and did drugs in front of her two young daughters.

But she was strong. Strong in confidence, and somehow still sweet and coy. She, and we, knew that she could manage any situation that came our way. Mom was busy and always had a job, usually more than one. She was fast and efficient. We were expected to do the same and keep up and do our part, as everyone had chores at the commune where we lived.

The commune was a self-proclaimed co-op, community, and childcare home. It wasn't a nudist colony or a large isolated country farm or any kind of cult with a charismatic leader. It was just our house. We weren't associated with a spiritual practice or any specific dogma. There was no prescribed set of rules that had to obeyed, and really, I don't recall any rules at all. The one prevailing spirit was to be nice to each other, to respect all things and all ways of life.

The commune provided 24/7 childcare for college students and other young parents in our university town looking for affordable babysitting solutions. The adults signed up for a shift to provide childcare coverage, and in trade their children could be dropped off, at any time, for any duration. Adults and kids came and went, but Mom, Lori, and I lived there full-time as our mom Paula was the one who coordinated it all.

Drug use was rampant. The adults stayed in an unsteady fog fueled by a wide assortment of available drugs—opium, mushrooms, cocaine, alcohol, ecstasy, and a four-inch orange ball of LSD stored in the freezer next to our popsicles, known as "Sunshine." The razor blade was kept handy, and they would slice a bit off of ol' Sunshine and trip throughout their designated childcare time slot. The LSD was constant but took a backseat to marijuana, their drug of choice.

The smell of pot consumed our clothes, our hair, and clung to our small grimy faces. That smoky cloud was as familiar to me as Mister Rogers might be to others. Instead of a Disney princess, the face on the Zig Zag rolling papers is a picture of my childhood. I still can see the dark blue outline of the character against the white background of the package. What a jolly fellow he was, always smiling at the users in the room.

The adults inhaled pot from pipes, bongs, hookahs, and expertly twisted up joints. They ate it in brownies, scrambled eggs, and baked it in cakes. The ingenuity of its use might make Martha Stewart proud, especially now with her side-kick Snoop Dogg.

The marijuana plant was savored, worshipped, and adored. If anything, this was their spirituality, maybe even what the co-op was founded on. They revered the entire process from growing and harvesting, to dry-ing, and the ritual of preparing to partake. A favorite tray, tucked furtively under the couch or just behind a book on a shelf, not out in the open, but always easily accessed, held a baggie of pot, lighter, rolling papers, and pipe. It was an all-purpose drug tray, with a lip or curved edge like an old-fashioned Coca Cola tray, and was good for lines of coke, baggies of 'shrooms or the sticky heavy wedge of opium. The razor blade that sliced off pieces of Sunshine was put to use laying out lines of coke or chopping particularly sticky wads of marijuana buds.

The pot ritual was sacred. I see it all so clearly in my memory and can recount each step like a tutorial: Begin by rolling a bud in your hands. This makes the seeds fall out to pitter-pat onto the tray. Then you tear the bud into manageable pieces, separating the bud from the stem. A straight edge, usually the Zig-Zag package flap, or razor blade, is used to push the pile up the tray, shifting your hands to get the seeds and heavier stem pieces to trickle down the tray. The seeds make pittle, pat, and plop noises as they roll down and collect into the curved edge of the tray. Shift, slide, roll, shift, slide, roll; the ritual continues while the seeds rattle against the metal.

This was the common scene at my home. The spirituality of the plant and the adults' utter conviction of the benefits of the drug held sway. I still see the motion of their hands. I hear the sounds of the seeds. I feel the focused effort, the repeat activity. The grown-ups sat around whomever was master of ceremonies preparing the joint, pipe, or hookah, anticipating the high, and we kids would smile and anticipate the smell and the fog that would envelope our world.

We all, adults and children, held the hippie vibe to be here now, now be here. We were carefree as we explored life and the fluid reality around us.

But it was not all Sunshine and roses. The drugs were plentiful and topped with free-flowing alcohol. Addictions formed. The adults staggered under the emotional weight of their minds, and they faltered in the "love all always" mantra. Fighting, anger, drama, sadness, and depression all took turns on the grown-ups of my world. That emotional roller coaster is never travelled alone, and we kids were along for the ride.

We witnessed plenty. Too much. The addiction and depression struggle finally beat one of the men who spent time at our home, and he hung himself from the tree in our front yard.[1] When he was discovered, one of the adults was supposed to usher us children out the back door so that we would not see the corpse. But we snuck into the front room and peeked through the window. We saw the dead body hanging limply against the pre-dawn sky, the dark tangle of Jesus hair loose across his face.

The air was completely still, inside and out. We children held our breath and simply stared. The body

---

[1] This scene is remembered differently by the children of the commune.

did not sway, like they do in the movies; it was motionless. We stood there huddled together and soaked in the scene. No rise and fall of his chest. No movement at all. His face was a pale shade of blue. He had no shirt on; his stained jeans covered his legs. The leaves were quiet. The steel grey clouds didn't move either. Everything was still.

He was not a father to any of the kids at the commune. He just hung out for the free love and the drugs and the love of drugs.

Now he hung heavy. He hung still.

Maybe we should push him, I thought morbidly. Push the body to see him swing, to create some movement in the yard, in the sky, anywhere.

I was just a little girl and I saw death that day, staring coldly at me. Every day we watched slow death occurring around us with drug use, but the evidence of a body silhouetted against the sky showed us death immediate.

The adult female, who was supposed to have prevented our seeing, found us and gathered us to her pant legs. She shooed us out the back door, and we trudged in our small group down the street to a neighbor's house. We walked past Rudi's bakery, where we always went for Long Johns. *Would I ever be able to eat a Rudi's Long John again without remembering the man in the tree?*

We snuck glances behind us, attempting to get a final glimpse at the body hanging in the yard. The older kids turned more frequently, but I was less adventurous and my coping skills were starting to form. My mind was already looking to the next adventure that we might be heading to. I was blocking the image from my mind and turning towards the future.

The adults in their purple haze failed us that day. But I didn't really know that then. Like any child, we only know what is. My mom and our life at the commune were my 'what is.'

The children of the commune banded together and moved through life as a unit, alternatively torturing and caring for each other. My sister Lori was one of the eldest in the group and a natural born leader.

Lori was strong, dirty, and relished being a tomboy. She rebelled at anything girly in those early years and was tough, true tough. Nothing fazed her. Lori bossed all the kids around, and we dutifully did her bidding. She would lead us to jump off the roof of a shed, play hide-and-go-seek in the cemetery, or ride our bikes down the potholed gravel alley in the backyard. She climbed every tree available and reigned supreme over the commune kids.

Lori was lean and muscular with a round face, like Mom's, often with a grimace or a sneaky smile. She looked angry all the time, but maybe that was because I annoyed her. Even her affection was violent. Noogies, indian burns, and a flat open slap to the back was the way she showed her love for me.

Meanwhile, much like mom, I was always smiling and laughing. I had white blond hair, piercing blue eyes, and was perpetually tan. I was goofy, lean, and ropey. We rode bikes, big wheels, and walked everywhere, or ran. I loved to run. I loved to feel my hair pulled backward by the force of the wind and the power of my legs, my body propelling me forward. I was always moving.

Lori carried herself with swagger, as most leaders do; she knew who she was and where she was going. She was quick with an order or a punch in the mouth. Lori defended us little ones when necessary. The adults were not always alert, so the leaders of the kid-pack had to watch out for the younger children. She also knew she had to keep me safe from the creepy men and my own naiveté.

We kids were mainly left to our own devices, and we had to work out our own problems. As one of the younger children in the brood, I was typically either left alone, forced into submissive role play, or manipulated to the interests of the older kids.

Teasing was constant, the threat and act of violence was only a moment away. I was used as a live doll, dressed up, hair cut, and made-up. I was marched into action and executed all my sister's orders. We put on plays for the adults, and I was the side character in all the scenes, playing the supportive role or physically acting out instructions.

In one performance, there was a scene from a Comet commercial. You might recall Comet, the green powdered caustic bathtub cleaner. The jingle we sang went like this:

"Comet—it makes your mouth turn green; Comet—it tastes like gasoline;

Comet—it makes you vomit; so go buy some Comet and vomit today!"

Once the jingle came to the end, I was to brush my teeth with a Comet-laden toothbrush. Purportedly, I was going to demonstrate the green mouth and the induced vomiting. As I moved the toothbrush to my mouth, one of the adults, through her drug-addled mind, thought to save me at the last moment, and she wrenched the toothbrush from my grasp. As she wrested it away at the final moment before it hit my lips, I began to realize the manipulation from the older children and what I would do to please them.

The adults were usually oblivious to the kid's activities. They were lost to their own world. The co-op arrangement was not only useful for getting high, but it also served to provide the next sex partner. The adults all seemed interchangeable to me, and it seems they were to each other as well, as they were partner-swapping during their childcare shifts. Night Care was a one stop shop of sex and drugs.

One night, Lori woke me up and took me into the hall. The older kids corralled us younger kids together and shushed us. They looked sternly in our eyes to make sure we knew they were serious and that we had to be quiet. We could not talk, giggle or let out a sound. We nodded and followed them down the narrow hallway.

I heard soft moans and quiet grunts. These sounds were not uncommon, but I had not seen the source of these noises before. We tiptoed down the hall and peeked around the doorframe into the edge of the living room. What filled my eyes blossomed confusion in my mind.

What were they doing?

There were multiple naked bodies strewn about the room. The adults were having an orgy on the living room floor. I saw dank dark patches of hair against pale skin. I stared at the twisted bodies, with hands reaching for someone else's nearby body part to rub. It seemed like everyone was moving to a unified rhythm. Maybe there was music playing, but in my memory, it is a silent scene.

Mouths, hands, breasts, nipples, penises, asses, vaginas, there seemed to be no boundaries; women and men and body parts and sticky hair. It all moved together in a tangle of sweat and humid pot smoke.

Their eyes were unseeing; some were half-lidded, some glittering, and some looked dull and flat. Mom's long black hair stuck to a wet body surface of a woman near her; her hair seemed to form a curtain covering an act with her mouth. Even at my young age, I felt pulled by curiosity and the tension in the air of an oncoming orgasm. I don't know how long we stood there, but the adults never realized we were there.

I'm not sure of the frequency of these group sex

sessions, but they occurred often enough to be remembered by the collective consciousness of the Night Care kids. We snuck back to our common sleeping area, and I felt insecure and unsafe. I know now that Maslow's Hierarchy of Needs starts with safety, shelter, and food. Safety was fleeting, with the adults tripping on acid and the kids governing themselves. Shelter and food would also prove inconsistent elements in our life.

"Hope? Hope!"

My speaker colleagues looked at me with raised eyebrows. "Are you okay?"

Obviously, my trip down memory lane was longer than the instant it felt like. I was back on the crowded sidewalk in Amsterdam smelling that marijuana smell and I wondered, not for the first time, how I had gotten here. Not this particular sidewalk, but this place in my life. *How was I delivering a symposium on sterility assurance in the pharmaceutical industry?*

DAY LILIES

Mom, Lori and I moved constantly. Mom said we moved so frequently because the landlords were unfair, raising the rent after we painted a room or some other ridiculous excuse. I know now the evictions were likely due to lack of payment, too many people in and out of the house, or too many neighbor complaints. The result was a prism of houses that we paraded through, temporarily made home, and then moved on. Lori and I estimated eleven houses by the time I was six.

The constant moving left me unsettled. Where would we be next week? Where would I play? Would there be food? Would the stove work? Would there be a bathroom? Where would we sleep?

The houses were usually bungalows, broken and sad on the bad side of town, fixer-uppers with drafty windows and scratched hardwood floors complete with small, cold bathrooms. The adult group would paint the inside of the new houses in DayGlo colors. We had the Yellow Submarine room, the Snuffleupagus room, and the Cookie Monster room. The garish colors assaulted the senses. The bright oranges and screaming yellows now seem like peering into a scary funhouse.

We always lived in houses, never apartments—probably too many close neighbors in an apartment. Mom always wanted a yard and a place to plant a garden for vegetables and her marijuana plants.

The actual house address changed with every move, but the co-op philosophy remained the same. Lori and I lived at the co-op, everyone else came and went, but it was our "home." Even so, we had little to no individual property, as everything was to be shared amongst the group. We had no personal items and no concerns. Clothes were interchangeable as long as they fit. Toys were shared too. There was no fighting over anything. Being one of the younger children with a deep desire to please, maybe I willingly gave and shared any items that may have been mine. I am not sure what the reality was. Maybe I had possessions, but because of the nature of the commune I did not see them as mine.

Material goods were simply shared with little definition of ownership.

Those lessons I find beneficial in some way, yet I had to learn what was considered acceptable elsewhere as I got older. My college roommate, God bless her soul, would get upset when I would borrow her clothes without asking. I would go into her closet and pick through her clothes with abandon. I had no concern and no reflection on the fact that these items were not mine. Jennifer was patient, kind, and willing to educate me on social norms that exist around property. She did have to draw the line when I loaned out her car to someone else. I had not even asked her. I told one of my friends that she could use my roommate's car. Who does that?! I was smart but still clueless in many areas. I did not know the value people place on items. People care for their material goods, and it is not socially acceptable to share someone else's stuff. I get it now (mostly).

Many people I know attach high value to their material goods, and they bolster it with a strong emotional component. Since I was raised in an environment where everything was shared, it was equally enjoyed, but was also easily released. I did not develop deep attachments to items. And honestly, that can be a good thing.

My childhood did include some consistency. We usually had a garden, although we never knew if we would be at that same house when it was time to harvest. But gardening was an essential part of our life, because it was a source of food. Every year we would plant corn, green beans, zucchini, summer squash, carrots, and lovely plump tomatoes. There is nothing more sublime than a warm, firm mid-August tomato from the vine, with the juice running down your chin. I would eat tomatoes until my mouth was full of acidic sores.

Every year mom would give Lori and me each a row in the garden to plant whatever we wished. Some years I would plant asparagus because it would come early, blessing me with the first harvest of the season. Some years Brussels sprouts, as they come late and we could savor the freshness until fall.

One year I planted a row of Tiny Tots, the miniature hard candies, in hopes they would grow candy bushes. Mom let me plant them. She let me go through the entire process of working the soil, planting the candy, and watering the row. This was a firsthand lesson I learned, that although she told me that it was candy and it would not grow anything at all, she let me prove to myself that candy does not grow into more candy.

Mom let me experience the process and discover the truth for myself. She was like that in all things; she did not thwart my curiosity. Mom fully supported the realm of experiences, and we were not curtailed in our efforts. The row of Tiny Tots did grow in the garden of my mind, revealing a deeper understanding of nature, my mom, and the good of the earth.

We always planted at least one or two rows of marijuana. Living in a southern Indiana college town, our bungalow neighbors were usually poor college students on their own drunken, drugged path. One summer two pot plants were stolen out of Mom's garden by the neighbor boys. Mom was outraged. We harvested the rest of the plants that day so they couldn't steal any more.

She enlisted my help. We cut them down at the base of the plant and hung them upside down from the two-by-four roughhewn oak rafters in the attic, spreading sheets over the asbestos insulation. The sheets would catch the "the shake" and the seeds as the plants dried. We walked carefully on the studs in the attic so we did not crash through the ceiling below. Mom was industrious and very possessive of her pot plants.

Our food was organic, which meant grown from our own garden (and fertilized by the sludge from the local electrical plant, which later was discovered to be PCB laden, but we're still here). Rice, potatoes, and vegetables were our staples. We rarely had anything with sugar, as these were "empty calories" and probably expensive. If things were especially lean, Lori and I were sent to the park for a harvest. The bungalows we lived in were usually situated near a park or a cemetery. Freedom in play could be found in these wide green spaces, and luckily dinner could be sourced there too.

My sister and I walked to the park and up a steep embankment to the railroad tracks. Orange daylilies consumed the hill, choking out all the other plant life, growing rampant for us to enjoy. The thick green undergrowth undulated in the afternoon sun. The bright flowers announced their delectableness. This would be dinner.

It was always a special day when we would get to eat flowers for supper. We had been convinced that this was exciting and was to be relished. Maybe intuitively we realized that we had no food, or money to purchase food—and down the road that may have led us to our different insecurities and eating disorders—but at the time we were enthralled with the idea of eating the daylilies that we picked.

We pinched the flowers at the base of the bloom, separating the bloom from the stem. We placed the whole bloom into the blue bucket with the broken handle that scratched the palm of my hand. Lori and I gathered a whole bucket full of orange blooms and trot home at a half skip, satisfied that we had done our part to feed the family.

At home Mom needed a bit of flour and a spoonful of fat. Mom was clever—she made it fun. This was a celebration, a treat! With a flourish, she tossed the fat into my great grandmother's cast iron skillet. The fat danced on the hot surface, the smell of grease filled the air, and my stomach tightened with the thought of oncoming food. Only then did I realize I was hungry. The blooms, properly dredged, would fry crunchy, tasty, and delicious.

Daylilies taste a little like grass, and a little like sunshine. Yes, they were something served for my belly to stave off the hunger, and they are also a happy memory for me. Mom was a good study, a capable gardener, even in the city confines, and she knew what urban plants were edible and could be eaten as needed. Mom put that knowledge to good use.

We did not go hungry often, but food was scarce and not reliable. The garden, the fresh vegetables, were a consistent source of sustenance. Safety, food, and shelter were at best unpredictable, but love and encouragement were in abundance. Mom loved us and we always knew that. She supported us, in her way. Life was far from ideal, but the commune was a place of pure acceptance and all were welcomed. What little we had, we shared. Until, of course, things changed.

BOX TOPS

I enter my numbers, card, and codes onto the keypad to get the prompt: Remove Nozzle. Select Fuel Type. Begin Fueling. *When did it start taking so long to actually begin pumping the gas?*

The fumes raise, and I turn my head to minimize the scent filling my nose and head. I stare unseeing into the gas station mini-mart. *Should I go in and get some scratch offs? Do I feel lucky today? Is the winning ticket waiting for me in there?*

I watch a burly dude walking out with a case of Bud Light under his left arm and a Diet Mountain Dew clutched in his right hand. He walks with purpose and direction. *He is probably going to have some fun today.*

The lever pops, pulling me out of my mind meanderings. I replace the pump and tighten the gas cap until it snaps. I firmly but gently press down the tank cover. I love my car, so I give it an extra pat.

I whoosh open my door and slide into the driver's seat. Brad looks at me at me and asks, "How much was it?"

"Huh?"

"How much did it cost?"

I return a blank stare.

"The gas, honey, the gas. How much was it?"

"Oh! I don't know."

In that moment, as I turn to peer at the pump to see the price, a realization tumbles into place: *I have made it!*

I just filled up my gas tank, and I have no idea how much it was. I don't know what the price per gallon is or the total cost. I did not have to stop and think about filling up instead of just putting in a few bucks of gas. I did not do any quick math or reflect on how much might be in my bank account. I just filled up my tank and got back into my car.

I have made it!

It does not seem all that long ago that filling up my tank was only on rare, flush occasions, usually after I got my tax refund. The majority of the time I would just put twenty dollars in the tank, not knowing the gallons, just the dollar amount. Twenty dollars was something I usually could afford.

This was the first true, unabashed moment that I realized what it meant, to me, to be "wealthy." To fill up the gas tank and not know how much it cost was an amazing feeling.

A second moment of realization came with a favorite school tradition of collecting Box Tops. In my previous life when the colored paper came home from school requesting Box Tops, it was summarily recycled because I knew I did not have any Box Tops, nor would I be collecting any to send to school.

Wal-Mart and Kroger generics don't have Box Tops. The difference between Kroger cake mix at seventy-two cents and Betty Crocker, with a Box Top, at eighty-two cents was significant enough to prevent the Betty Crocker purchase. Now I can spend the extra ten cents on the Betty Crocker cake mix to donate to the school through the Box Top program. I will admit that my pantry is still full of Great Value food items, but so too is my Box Top collection baggie. I dutifully send in ours to the school every month. And I assume

I am the only mom in the school who feels wealthy in being able to do so.

I shared my Box Top story with my mother-in-law one day, and she, quite sensibly, asked, "You did not realize you had made it when you moved into this house?" *Right,* I think, *the house I live in is a clear sign that we are doing well.* I forgot about that.

For me, the small things somehow feel much more significant. My husband had a milestone goal of a big house and recognized its significance when we moved in, but my own realization of success has come in the smaller moments.

My husband's perception is helpful in other ways too. He opens my eyes to options that I do not even see. Several years into our marriage, he asked me why I always wear the same bra. I went into a lecture about how little he knows about women.

"Brad, women only wear their one favorite bra," I instructed. "All women have one bra for daily wear and one or two for nice or special occasions," I stated matter-of-factly. "It is about the fit. This one is a Victoria's Secret Demi style."

"Don't they come in different colors?" he asked.

"Do they have more than just black Victoria's Secret Demi?"

"Of course."

"Then why don't you buy the same style in different colors?"

"Well …" I stammered. "Um, I mean, they are expensive. It would be expensive to buy more than one color or one bra."

"Babe," he flashed me a playful grin. "Why don't you go and get one for every day of the week in all the colors that they sell? Get different colors, patterns, whatever." He paused for effect. "I think you should have more than one bra."

Right. Right, I thought to myself. *I will get bras in every color. I won't wear the same one every day.* The thought had never occurred to me, that I could buy more than one bra at a time. But I can. I can go to Victoria's Secret and buy more bras.

SPILLED MILK

My giggle bubbled up inside of me. Lori had made a joke. I was quick to laugh and, once started, it's hard for me to stop. But the timing was awful. At the dinner table with Mom, her new husband, Nicoli, and his three kids, laughing was not allowed, unless of course it was for something witty that Nicoli said.

Every dinner now was formal with assigned seats, napkins on laps, and rigid rules for manners that would make a military boarding school seem like a breeze and the commune a lost dream.

I clamped my mouth shut as I took a big gulp of milk. The giggle tickled my throat, threatened and teased, as my body shook trying to contain the laughter. The force and pressure proved too much, and the milk squirted out my nose.

All five kids erupted at my milk explosion and

doubled over in laughter with me. However, my glee was short-lived. I managed a furtive glance at Nicoli, and his look told me to rein it in, this behavior was too much. This type of unbridled joy was just too loud, too much fun, and not proper dinner decorum. I knew I had to shut up and get my area cleaned up fast.

In my haste to mop up the nose-milk, I knocked over the large pitcher of milk on the table. It raced across the smooth, white oak surface, flowing under the edges of the plates and serving bowls, sneaking under the fear and anger that was sure to follow.

There was a collective pause at the table. All the kids knew what a spill meant, and they all knew they could catch trouble for laughing. Spilled anything was never good, but with all of the laughter too? Too much. Mom leveled her eyes at me and—with a quick twitch of her eyebrows—let me know she loved me, but I was on my own.

"What have you done? Why would you do that?" Nicoli bellowed.

Head down, hands in lap, I mewled, "It was an accident."

"If you weren't such a clumsy slob, this would not have happened!" he screamed.

Not uttering a word, as I knew it better not to say anything, I moved slowly trying to sop up the milk with my napkin, glancing at him from the corner of my eye.

"Just stop and go to your room," Nicoli commanded, slamming his fist on the table with a shuddering boom.

I stood up from the table and stepped over the enormous, heavy white oak bench. Having to pass behind Nicoli, I inhaled, trying to make myself flat and invisible and skirt around the edge of the room. As I slinked down to the basement, the open-rise stairs echoed under my footsteps, the avocado-colored carpet mats doing nothing to dull the noise of my steps as the dining room remained silent.

My "bedroom," if you could call it that, was an area in the bare, grey, unfinished block wall basement. My twin mattress was on the concrete floor, from which the cold seeped in from the ground. I had a well-worn and marred dresser that we had rescued from someone else's trash. I had tried to decorate it with a million tiny red apple stickers, but it still looked sad. My lime green throw rug made an attempt at cheer, but failed against the dark cold space.

My dog, Pups, slept with me, and the bed was

covered in black dog hair, flea nits, and heavy white pet dander. My thin sheets, lumpy pillow, and flimsy blanket were not exactly welcoming but felt better than the yelling upstairs. I crawled into my grimy safety nest and sobbed, loudly.

I wailed into my pillow, loud and hysterical. "It was an accident!" I kept repeating. "I didn't mean to be clumsy. I would have cleaned it up. It was an accident."

With wet face and sticky nose, I cried and rambled on out loud, louder than I knew I should be, but I wanted my family to know my pain. I wanted them to know my anguish and feel sorry for me. I should not be outcast from the family and sent away for spilling milk.

Laughing too hard had gotten me into trouble, and now crying too loud was going to do the same. My intent was not to bring further wrath, only to let them know. I just wanted them to hear me.

I hoped Mom would come down to comfort me, but the truth inside of me knew that was impossible. Mom would be pegged to the bench by the force of Nicoli's glare. She would not be allowed to comfort me. She would not be allowed to move. She would only be allowed to work on cleaning up the stray liquid that had spread on the grand table. No, Mom would not be joining me down in my dank dungeon. So I bawled and carried on, hiccupping my sorrows into the dingy pillow.

Boom, boom, boom. I heard footsteps overhead. Heavy steps heading towards the basement stairs. I gulped, swallowed the tears, and sucked myself into silence. I peeked from my pillow. *Oh Shit.*

Nicoli raced down the ugly avocado stairs.

"Stop crying! Why are you fucking crying? Are you a baby? You are the one who made the fucking mess! Stop crying! The whole family, the whole dinner, is ruined because of you."

Balled up on the grungy mattress, wide-eyed and afraid, breathing hard and sobbing, but attempting to hold it in, I didn't respond. I knew better. No response ever sufficed; better just to be quiet, be small, and wait.

"ENOUGH!" he growled.

Nicoli pounced on the mattress and kneeled into me. His knee pressed into my hip and side. He grabbed my shirt collar and pulled my face to his.

"Enough! Why can't you stop fucking crying? Is there something wrong with you? Are you fucking re-tarded? Are you that fucking stupid? Can you hear me?"

He shook me with each demand. His face purple with rage, his arms ready for violence, his spittle splashed my face.

"WHY CAN'T YOU STOP CRYING?"

His fists clenched into my shirt. He thrust me back into the pillow with each declaration of stupidity. I remained silent, blinking back my tears. My eyes met his, my lips pressed shut. I did not dare him with a direct stare, but I saw him. I saw his rage and crystal blue eyes in his contorted face.

Silent and shivering, I waited. I waited for the blow that would come next. I tensed for the explosion of pain and looked forward to the quiet that would come after.

RED VELVET

Nicoli was king of his castle, a perfectionist, and loved to cook. Like all the meals he prepared and all the activities in which he participated, Nicoli took his time to do it well, to savor the process as well as the finished product. His ratatouille took two days to prepare to his acceptance. After the hours of preparation, a smug satisfaction played across his face as he watched us all "ooh" and "ahh" as we sampled the smooth red sauce clinging to the eggplant, zucchini, mushrooms, onions, and squash.

All work was done for praise. Nicoli loved to be the center of attention. His ego was enormous, like his handmade table and benches where we sat for dinner. Thick white oak, sturdy and ostentatious in size and structure, demanding attention like its builder. The dining set was too big for the room, so we skirted around the edges of the room, as we skirted around his personality.

Nicoli stood at the head of the table each night at dinner and undressed. He removed all his clothes, carefully folding his shirt, pants, and socks, until he got down to his Speedo-style underwear. He posed there, with only his bikini underwear, for us to admire. A marathon runner and avid fan of exercise, he delighted in showing off his well-muscled, early-middle-aged body. He lifted weights and was enthralled with the shape, form, and color of his body. For the rest of the evening, the man moved around the house in his tight bright blue panties, eager to show his muscles and bulge off to the world.

One of my friends once asked, "Why does your dad not wear any clothes?" I merely shrugged. I had no answer. He just didn't. It's amazing what becomes normal to a child, and I had not known much normalcy in my young life.

Nicoli was a son of Polish immigrants and wore his Slavic ethnicity as a badge of honor. A tenured quantum physics professor at the university, he had a towering intellect. He was also a narcissistic egomaniac who knew how intelligent and powerful he was.

Quick to let you know his IQ and how important and groundbreaking his work was, he taught us about quarks and particle physics. Our home played host to world-renowned physicists, Russian, German, Polish, and other Americans, drinking vodka, arriving with gifts for my mother, and she, in turn, would share her knowledge of rolling a joint.

A high-functioning alcoholic, Nicoli drank a case of Miller Lite every couple of days. Along with his alcoholic biting wit came the violence and bursts of anger. He expected everyone to be as smart, as conscientious, and as much of a perfectionist as he was. He was quick to anger, slow to accept, and loath to admit faults. Nicoli demanded obedience and blind acceptance of his authority. His huge ego dominated our world and all the needs of the house.

Their marriage immediately followed our co-op life. We went from a formless, amorphous existence filled with free love to a painful extrusion into shape, structure, discipline, and rigor. Lori and I went from largely managing ourselves to conforming to a specific mold of children who were to be seen, not heard—only speaking when spoken to. Here, stability was not only established, but we were forced to choke on it. Dishes had to be washed and dried a certain way, toys were not to be exposed, and sharing ideas or a conflicting opinion was frowned upon.

Dinners were every night, on the dot, a formal affair, with Nicoli barely dressed at the head of the table that was properly set with plates, napkins, silverware, and that damned pitcher of milk. Discussions could be held quietly, as long as they did not interrupt the dinner. Everyone was expected to maintain a level of quiet decorum, which largely consisted of listening to Nicoli talk about himself or his work.

He and Mom had met in the physics department at the university. Mom had gotten a job as his secretary, good at typing, organizing, and with that underlying sexual appeal that left her never lonely. She must have been gravitating towards structure, eager for some predictability in our lives. Maybe she was finally seeing the destruction of the co-op. The nation too was moving in this direction, looking for more order and ending the hippie days. Maybe she was just hungry.

Mom fell in love easily, she loved deeply, and when she committed to something, she did it with fervor. She chose this man to marry, falling for his impressive physique, commanding presence, and his intellect.

Mom holds her own in intelligence. She never finished university, due to drugs and distractions, but she has a raw intellect that is clear, decisive, and holds its own authority. But the demands of this new environment of order, discipline, and anger distracted her to a new sort of neglect. Mom fell into the shadow of Nicoli's personality and disappeared from Lori and me. She was no longer lost to the ongoing drug use and fucking on the living room floor, but she married a man who was impossible to please, and she emotionally withdrew.

He took her power by making her small, belittling her. He called her names. Lazy. Idiot. Stupid hillbilly. She became immobilized, cornered, so badly wanting to please him. We were now secure in a home, with personal possessions and we were fed regularly, but Mom was not available. She now had five kids to manage, a full-time job, and a high-maintenance husband. Add in the violence and abuse, and truly she was unable to be the mother she wanted to be. Every family member in a home where abuse occurs develops coping mechanisms, some good and some bad. I now understand how hard this time must have been for her. She did try her best, and she did love us unconditionally. Mom gave us as much time as she could, but Nicoli demanded more from her.

I was still young when the relationship started, but Lori was older and the environment and new demands bridled against Lori's nature. Our new step-siblings were two boys and a girl. I was the youngest out of all of us. We first moved to a squat yellow bungalow near the university with a limestone front porch and a sweet porch swing. His children were there only part-time, but they were given the bedrooms. Their rooms were complete with wood floors, beds, dressers, end tables, painted drywall, posters, and hung pictures.

Lori was relegated to one corner of the unfinished basement. She did have a bed though, my great-grandma's iron frame double bed. Lori had a purple fuzzy throw rug on the cold, cracked concrete floor. The only light was a naked bulb hanging on the wood rafters. Her cat, Boots, with whom she shared a mutual-worship relationship, always kept her company and caught the mice in her basement room.

In this house, I had a room of sorts on the main floor. It was a converted back kitchen, eight by eight feet square, with a non-functioning sink and broken wall cabinets. Mom installed a piece of plywood atop the counter and sink, and placed my mattress on top. I had a room. My own room. My bed. My pillow. My blanket. It was constantly cold, but I thought it a fine little room, the smallness was safe and secure. It was my room, and it was good.

Although a secure place to sleep was nice, my insecurity about our home showed up in other ways. I began to wet the bed. Maybe it was the constant moving, maybe it was the new world order of Nicoli, maybe it was the yelling and violence, but for whatever reason I woke up many mornings with a wet bed. I was embarrassed, and the taunting of the other kids only made it worse.

I woke up sticky, cold, and wet. The smell wafted through my room. I didn't want to go into Mom's room again and tell them what I had done. I peeled off my pajamas and pulled my sheet and blanket from my bed, thankful that Mom had me sleep on a rubber sheet to protect my cranky mattress on the plywood. Just as I was getting the nerve to carry my bundle down to the washer, Mom came in.

With hand on her hip, she cocked her head and frown-smiled at me.

"Oh, honey. Again?" she chirped.

I let out a big sigh and searched her face pleadingly.

"It's all right, baby. We'll get through this." She scooped up the sheets from my arms. "We've just got to make a plan. A goal. That's all." She trotted off down the stairs.

"But Mom, I don't know what's wrong with me," I whined as I followed her into the basement. "I don't even wake up after I pee. I sleep right through it then lay in it all night," I pouted.

"Well, Hopey, I'm sure we'll figure it out. The doctor said nothing is wrong with you physically, so we will have to figure something else out."

Mom was loving and accepting; she never yelled at me or made me feel small. Her positivity perked me up. She started to teach me visualization and meditation techniques. I had to visualize the bathroom and would dream about a bathroom when I had to pee.

Then she set up a reward system for me. She put a gold-star-sticker chart on the refrigerator. The reward for thirty days in a row with no wet bed was a new outfit; specifically, I wanted a pair of red sweatpants with my name on the butt and white sweatshirt with the university logo. I was excited. I wanted those sweatpants!

The downside to the sticker chart was that everyone knew every morning of my success or failure in the night. The first week I had one accident, then after that never again. I only missed one day of placing a gold star on the chart. Mom's technique worked. I did thirty nights in a row without wetting the bed. In the process I learned about goal setting, tracking progress, being solutions-focused, and exploring methods to improve. Mom consistently taught me these skills, which have proven successful for me later in life.

The step-siblings hated my sticker chart. They hated my mom for breaking up their parents' marriage. They hated Lori and me too. When the blended family first happened, Lori and I had just come from the commune, up for anything, willing to play along and be friends and not much seemed strange to us. Yet intuitively, we felt lingering pain and cruelty in these three kids.

They were bullies, unfriendly, unwelcoming, and openly violent. They were extremely rough with each other, causing deep purple and green bruises to appear on their pasty skin, arising in inappropriate places, with bite marks lining their inner thighs. The younger two were the most mean-spirited, products of their father's quick anger and caustic wit. They were close in age and extremely small in stature; maybe that was part of the reason for their rage and hatred. Their father wore them down with alcohol-infused fury and violence. The eldest boy was quieter; he could hold his own in anger, but mostly only fought with his siblings and was content to leave Lori and me alone.

Coming from an environment of free love and acceptance, these children seemed evil to me. As the youngest, I was good for constant teasing and belittling, but when it came to the physical acts of violence, I was too young and would cry too loud. They hated me, but they largely left me alone.

Lori was a challenge to them, an unknown. They engaged in acts of terror on her, which was easy in her basement bedroom. Well-placed dead mice, rumors of ghosts, hiding and stealing her things were their first attempts at trickery. Lori was tough, though. Unable to get the desired reaction from my unfazed sister, they continued to ratchet up their methods of torture. Then Boots, her cat, disappeared. His body was never found, and we all knew he had not run away. Lori was devastated. She fought valiantly, but Thing 1 and Thing 2 were never formally accused, as Nicoli would not allow it. He didn't care that the cat was gone. The kids did despicable things to other animals, so why not Boots? It was a twisted way of getting their jollies and success-fully tormenting Lori. Lori knew what had happened to Boots, I assumed, and Mom pretended it was untrue.

I was no match for these deranged children, but Lori could hold her own. Her street smarts and analyt-ical mind served her well in the competition for child dominance. However, she became as hateful as they were. The transition to the order and structure of this new household was painful for us all, and Lori's coping mechanism was anger. She hated Nicoli from the be-ginning. It was not easy for her to move into discipline and rigor from a life of unfettered fun and lawlessness.

Besides a mandated dinner time and strict etiquette, Lori now had a curfew, had to do homework, and had to obey rules. We were no longer part of the fabric of existence of free love, and we were not accepted for who we were. Nicoli's love was doled out sparingly and lashed with pain.

Lori had been free and strong at the co-op, as she was one of the oldest kids. Lori had power and was the leader. Her instincts were valuable in leading the Night Care kids, however that intelligence was not admired now. She was constantly belittled about her intellectual capabilities. She got Cs in school and was not academically inclined.

Nicoli favored academics. He constantly quizzed us and gave us riddles, promoting the children in the house with academic prowess and good grades. Lori was compared to the other siblings, who had been raised with intellectual promotion, and she did not perform as well. She was, however, highly observant, analytical, and curious. These strengths gave her a profound awareness of the changes we had been subjected to and a deeper impact of the anger and violence. Yet her power had been stripped. Physically, too, she was removed from the family, relegated to the basement—dark, dank, and unfriendly. Her physical environs matched the social confines she was now faced with. Lori was deeply aware of the dichotomy between our old life and the differing living standards with Nicoli and his kids. As she struggled to adjust, she became the brunt of our new family's anger and pain.

Lori was the reason for any discord. The violence-laden, unhappy home had to have a scapegoat, and Lori was ours. Any trouble in the house, no matter if it was started by the evil-two or anyone else, somehow was to be blamed on Lori. Like any child in that situation might do, she began to embrace and exploit her role as the family troublemaker.

Her acting out started small at first, not washing the dishes the specified way or setting the table inaccurately. She refused to do her chores, clean her room, or do her homework. She blasted angry music—AC/DC, Motley Crue, Judas Priest, and Dio. She railed against the parents, angry, hurt, and lonely. Lori was searching for love and affection, which didn't come from our family unit. So she found it elsewhere.

Lori started dating a boy named Jacob. He was eighteen and drove a DeLorean, one that the men of the house drooled over. My sister was just twelve years old, but even at that young age, she was full grown, with full hips and booty, curly hair, and gorgeous smile, which she rarely offered. Lori carried the swagger and sexuality of our mother. Jacob was handsome, dark skinned with high cheek bones, a beautiful, smarmy young man who knew how to manipulate a young girl's mind.

Adrift and lonely, aching for the love and acceptance she had known before, Lori stole Miller Lites from the fridge and snatched pot from Mom's bedside table, but her actions went unnoticed. Her escapades escalated. One weekend, while Mom was out of town with Nicoli, Lori's actions ended her up in a stolen car at the police station. Mom had to cut her California trip short and collect Lori from wherever she was.

Finally, this action was big enough to get Mom's attention, who now became fully focused on "retraining" Lori. Our mother was convinced she could do what it took to get Lori under control and to obey the rules. The first and only reprogramming session took place in our living room. Mom sat on the blood-red velvet couch next to the slate-topped end tables and placed an array of objects on the floor. Lori sat in a yellow furry chair that rotated in a circle.

Mom stepped Lori through a series of questions: What is your name? Where do you live? How do feel today? Then she attempted to command Lori through a series of instructions and have her do a task. Hand me the napkin. Take the napkin from me. Hand me the plate. Take the plate from me. Hand me the knife.

Lori refused each step. She would not engage. She would not listen. She sat and slowly spun in the golden chair. Lori refused to hand Mom the objects or take them from her. Mom kept on with the demands. Lori then started throwing things at Mom and trying to wrest others from her hands.

The tension grew into full-blown rage. Both screamed, red-faced, breathless. Mom went on, unrelenting in the demands.

"Hand me the plate, Lori."

Lori ignored her.

"Hand me the plate."

Lori spun in her chair.

"You must be able to take direction. You must do what I say."

"Fuck you, you stupid bitch!" came Lori's response. "I am not handing you the fucking plate; get it your fucking self." Lori spun in the chair, half snarling, fully glaring.

Mom took a calming breath. "You cannot speak to me that way," Mom replied, her voice with only a slight quiver.

"I am not handing you anything, Mom. You can get it your fucking self or just fuck off."

"YOU MUST HAND ME THE PLATE, Lori!"

Lori didn't flinch. Her chair finished its cycle, and her eyes came to rest on the knife. I am not sure why the knife was brought out with the other items. Was it to entice? Was it to invite a bigger struggle, to provide a weapon that could do real damage, real harm?

I had been watching from the dining room, standing in the doorway, not entering the living room. I could not let the knife get involved. I took a step into the living room.

"Stop it, Mom," I whimpered as I started to cry. The lump in my throat prevented a strong voice. "Someone is going to get hurt." I was afraid of the knife, afraid of what would happen if Mom didn't let up. "Mom, just leave Lori alone."

"This is none of your business, Hope." Mom turned only her eyes to me, her face and body remained trained on Lori. "You need to stay out of it."

"I won't. You can't do this, you can't scream at her all the time, you have to stop treating her this way." I was crying hard now, and I forced my words past a curtain of tears and snot.

"What do you expect? What do you think I should do? Do you think it's okay for her to have the police calling me?" Mom retorted, now fully facing me. Her turning away from Lori was enough, enough to break the tension and whatever evil spell had settled in the room.

Lori slammed out the front door. Mom stood up, dusted imaginary lint off her pants and gathered up the materials of her training. Her mouth pressed into a flat line; she didn't look or respond to me. She carried the items into the kitchen, put them away, and started making dinner.

Left unchecked, I know Lori and Mom would have hurt each other. Our roles were now cemented. Lori was there to bring anger, Mom was there as much as she could be, and I was to be the peacemaker.

7000 SQUARE FEET

"**D**o you like it?" Brad asks me, as he searches my face for clues.

"Hmmm," I stall, not really wanting to tell my husband what I'm thinking.

The realtor frets, bouncing her glances between us. Brad loves the place, and she knows it. She also senses my hesitation, as a good realtor can. She wisely steps away as we make our return to the enormous kitchen.

"What is it, honey?" Brad asks.

"I don't know." I hesitate some more. "It's nothing. There is nothing wrong with the house. It's beautiful."

"I know, right?" he grins. Then my husband looks at me, still seeing reservation. "Well, then what is it? What's wrong?"

"It's just so big!" I blurt out. "I mean, how do you take care of a house like this? I will spend my life trying to keep up!" My fears feel like they pour out of my mouth right onto the gleaming floor.

"Oh, honey, you won't have to clean it," Brad states so obviously. "We'll get a housekeeper." He places his hands on my shoulders, reassuring me that I would not have to clean this monstrosity.

It's a simple solution for him. I, on the other hand, had not even considered that as a possibility. A house-keeper? *How absurd. Who has a housekeeper?*

The home is 7,000 square feet of finished space with a four-car garage and four flag poles. Yes, four flag poles. Fourteen-foot-high ceilings, imported Brazilian cherry floors, handmade custom cherry cabinets, including the refrigerator, dishwasher, and place to hide the trash receptacles. The library and the living room have a fancy ceiling with more imported Brazilian cherry, beautiful in height and complexity. The kitchen has a 100-square-foot food pantry with a frosted glass door stating, "Pantry." The pantry is bigger than most of my bedrooms growing up.

The entryway takes my breath away, with the largest door known to man, the front stairs are more Brazilian cherry with views into the living room and formal dining space. The graceful back stairs lead to the kitchen again. It is awe inspiring and quiet honestly intimidating.

We bought it.

It takes me weeks, if not months, to not be confused when I drive into my own driveway. *Who the hell lives in a house like that?* Oh right, that is mine. This is where I live.

I was a single mom for many years before I met Brad. I ran a lean home, and we lived well within my means. I owned my home and two cars, had zero debt (except student loans). I was making six figures on my own, but we lived efficiently and inexpensively. We had a modest home, decent clothes, and were not hungry. I had never dreamed of a big home; it was just not a goal for me.

I am guided by career goals and defined success that way. I like to make a difference by improving processes, systems, profits or reducing inefficiencies. That drive is how I excel at work and aligns with my natural approach to life. I do not like waste or things that are inefficient, and that was reflected in our modest lifestyle.

Brad, however, did have the dream of a big house. So here we are.

I also had no experience in my childhood, or

adulthood for that matter, that prepared me for the undertaking of decorating a large house.

We started with the seemingly simple task of "window treatments." I don't understand why they are not called curtains; I guess when you live in a big house, they are called window treatments. And "window treatments" were my first hurdle in this new experience. We have forty-eight huge, custom-built windows, which eliminates heading to Wal-Mart to buy plastic blinds—my approach to "window treatments" before.

Stores don't carry the custom sizes we need, and every curtain/blind/decorating company expects to come out during the day to "partner" with "the woman of the house" on her "window treatment" choices. *What is this? The 1950s?*

I arrange a time for the salesman to come to the house. I am a successful career woman, leading huge departments of people, running projects, and managing multi-million-dollar budgets, yet there are things out of my knowledge base. *Do I want valances, curtains, shades, portiere, shutters, veils, jalousies, venetian blinds, drapes, oleos? What fabrics? Colors? Did I have a "theme"?*

Theme? What the hell does that even mean?

Growing up, we mostly used sheets or old table-cloths to cover our windows.

The sales guy hands me piles of samples and books to look through. His questions are probably normal to him, but come out as a bizarre barrage of phrases I am unfamiliar with. "Do you have a tone, style, or status that you would like to portray? Where is your color pallet?"

Bewildered and overwhelmed, I start to get angry.

Theme? Tone? Status? What? Who even talks like this?

Then I look at the prices. I am floored; I do not want to buy a single item. I spent less on my first three cars than one set of curtains he wants to sell me for my dining room.

Brad saves me. He overhears from the kitchen and comes in and sits down at the table. He makes the decision to put three-inch wood blinds in all the windows, except the master bedroom and bath, which will have some sort of shade. Brad takes care of it all in fifteen minutes. The sales guy goes off to measure all of the windows. Brad wraps his arms around me and chuckles.

"I got this, Babe." He smiles and leans into my hair. "Window treatments are easy."

Pfft. Window treatments.

Next up we have to finish the bathrooms. We have to get towel bars and toilet paper holders. I suggest Wal-Mart. Brad suggests Home Depot and Lowes. I never had to buy a towel bar before, and to this day I hope I don't ever have to do it again. Do you know how much they cost? And forty dollars for a bathroom trashcan is unbelievable! A miniature trashcan? Why is it forty dollars?

The Goodwill has good stuff at decent prices; let's just shop there. I still shop there.

Although my net worth has changed, my feelings are the same. As a child, I did not want people to judge me by the home I lived in. It is the same now. I do not want people to judge or categorize me by the home I live in.

The big home does not define me. My bathroom trashcans do not define me. Nor do window treatments.

FERMILAB

Life under Nicoli's rule became my new norm. I never really knew Mom's first husband, Lori's dad. Mom had married her much older boyfriend when she was sixteen and pregnant with Lori. That's what got her to this college town; he was going to university, and she came here to join him. The marriage didn't last long. Mom was back to taking care of herself, like she was born knowing how to do, and now she had a baby.

My father was her second husband. I don't know all the details, but they married when she was twenty. My dad was doing PhD work at the university and got into the craziness of the drug culture of the time too. They married and split quickly. I was three weeks old when they divorced. So Mom was still in her twenties when she married Nicoli, Husband number three. She would go on to have four more husbands. My dad went on to explore five marriages in total.

I hadn't minded commune life because I didn't know much else, but in truth I gravitated towards stability, security, and predictability. Life under Nicoli's roof was far from a peaceful sanctuary, but I adapted. Maybe I take that from my mom—adaptability.

I enjoyed the intellectual puzzles and quizzes Nicoli offered; they gave my mind something to work on, something to figure out, a problem to solve. Something concrete, safe, and predictable. I love numbers, and the security of numbers holds true with me today.

Even though the fear of anger and violence loomed over us, I even sort of enjoyed dinners at the table. The stability of this new life outweighed the fear and anger. A volatile environment was comfortable for me because it was introduced at a time in my life that predictable food and shelter were also secured.

Oblivion was my escape and my coping mechanism. I pretended to not know what was going on or chose to ignore it, and this protected my psyche. I liked the predictable dinners, the sturdy table, and the place to sleep. Nicoli's explosions were less scary with time. We, the whole family, knew when they were coming.

We knew what the rules were and when the rules were stretched too thin; everyone knew what was coming next.

I also gained ground with Nicoli; maybe it was because I was the youngest, but I also now believe it was because of my intellect. He challenged me with different puzzles, scenarios, and tests, and I was good at them. One night at dinner, he issued me a challenge around measuring time. He asked me to tell him when three minutes had passed, without looking at a watch or counting out loud. I took on the little test, and the family went on talking around me. I started to talk and add to the discussion at the table.

He tilted his head at me, "Be careful. If you start talking, you won't be able to keep time. Don't forget about the test."

"Okay," I replied. "I can do it."

I was confident I could do both. I talked with the family and kept time in my head in the background of mind.

"Three minutes is up." I looked at Nicoli.

He looked at his watch. "Only four seconds off. Impressive."

He was surprised that I was only four seconds off

while maintaining a conversation. Winning these little games earned me respect from him. I played chess with Nicoli too. I never won but held my own for my age and was highly teachable.

During summers, Nicoli worked at Fermilab, the now-defunct particle accelerator in the Chicago suburbs. The whole family would haul up there in our silver Subaru station wagon, joining other tenured professors' families. We stayed in one of the orange, blue, or red houses, all exact duplicates. It reminded me of *A Wrinkle in Time,* where all the houses are the same, all the children are playing ball the same, all happening at the same time.

The summer when I was eight-going-on-nine, Nicoli and I made the trip alone. My dad lived in Wisconsin and was meeting us there to pick me up for a month-long summer visit. There were patches of time in my growing up when I saw my dad in the summer and sometimes over the winter holiday break.

I was happy to go visit my dad and was actually happy to be alone in the car with my step-dad. There was no one to fight with me or pick on me. The six-hour trip with Nicoli flew by with discussions about physics, math, philosophy, and other challenges. I showed a natural curiosity for physics and what he did. I, in no real way, understood particle physics, but he appreciated my interest and my questions. Clearly, I was too young for any real intellectual exchanges, but Nicoli saw a capability and a raw intelligence in me. After this trip, I held a different position in the home, and specifically with Nicoli.

After that trip, I could interject and represent for Lori or Mom in arguments, or at least break up the argument and get them to move on to something else. Not only arguments between Mom and Lori, but between Nicoli and Mom too. I got adept at de-escalating situations and removing the spotlight from the victim for a bit. This helped me in my own comfort with the anger and violence because I was developing tools to ratchet down the emotions in the room and get people to move on.

The goal was to find solutions with the least amount of anger, pain, and violence, solutions that would let everyone save face. Never could I have foreseen how being solutions-oriented would serve me so well later in life and how my upbringing shaped my ability to create order out of chaos, the skillset I use to create success in my career now. In a twisted way, I'm grateful for the Nicoli years.

The following summer when I was at my dad's (with his fourth wife, Rita), my mom called Rita to let them know that she and Lori had moved out and were staying with friends. Mom had left Nicoli. She had had enough. I don't know what happened to prompt her to finally leave, but crazy as it seems, I didn't like the news.

Rita and Dad sat me down and broke the news to me gently. I was floored, surprised, and crushed. Certainly, I knew Mom and Nicoli fought all the time, but I had grown used to it and thought that was just the way it was to be. I didn't know the depths of anguish my mom experienced; I was only a kid. I had grown comfortable with this family dynamic. I enjoyed the stability provided, even with the violence.

"I want to go home," I told Dad and Rita.

"Why?" Rita asked matter-of-factly.

"To get them back together," I stated, as if it was the most obvious thing in the world.

"How are you going to do that?"

"I don't know, but I know I can do it."

Rita and my dad worked on convincing me that

there was nothing I could do to save the marriage. Plus, my mom had already moved out. Rita urged me to accept my new reality. What she didn't know and couldn't understand was my fear of going to yet another temporary home, with no place to call my own. Even though life with Nicoli was far from perfect, there was predictability. There was a routine and rhythm to the days. I didn't want disruption.

That night, two days before my tenth birthday, was marked by a hot August thunderstorm. I wore a dress Rita had sewn for me that looked and felt like a stiff curtain, heavy scratchy cotton, blue flowers on a green background with an embellished neckline. My bowl-cut blond hair curled around my soon-to-be ten-year-old face.

Before the phone call from Mom, we had been celebrating my oncoming birthday, as I would not be there for the actual day. They had given me my gift, three-foot-long red ribbed plastic tubes. When you swung the tubes in circles, they whistled a low constant hum. After the phone call, I felt lost and unmoored. I couldn't stop my tears. Rita urged me to let it go, to let my feelings flee from within me. So we ran.

We ran outside into the warm night, the heavy rain

flattened our hair against our heads. We crossed the busy street and escaped to a wide-open green space. We danced in the rain. We raged with the thunder. I twirled that plastic tube to the low hum as quickly and consistently as I could, as the rain tried to beat out the sound. I screamed at the dark sky and welcomed the water into my upturned mouth. I cried for the loss of another home; albeit violent, it was predictable. I cried for my childhood, who I was, and to the unknown of where we were going next. I cried for my pain, which I couldn't truly comprehend. My sobs were drowned out by the pouring rain, the rolling thunder, and the hum of red plastic tubes.

DONUTS

A sweet yeasty smell filled the small kitchen with the warmth and inviting aroma of baking donuts. Sticky dough rising, glaze melting, that delicious odor wafted out the oven door. We made these donuts every morning. They came frozen, in a large black box, a dozen blocks of unhealthy sustenance and sugar. Obviously, things had changed again.

First thing I did when waking up was go to the kitchen to preheat the oven, then start getting ready for school. Heading back to the bedroom I shared with Mom, I would leap over the giant heating vent in the center of our house. The four-by-four vent in the living room floor was effective at heating the 800-square-foot house. The clumpy slate-blue carpeting edged too close to the vent and slightly overlapped the outdoor carpeting in the kitchen. The vent could not be walked on lest I burn my feet. Mom's tennis shoes melted one day when she put them there to dry.

The last slow vestiges of winter clung to the thin light of the morning. The grey sun filtered in quietly through the grimy window into our tiny home. The house felt snug in its smallness, the baking donuts, and the quiet movements of the morning.

I made my "bed" every morning, the narrow cushion that folded up into a chair during the day and was a sleeping mat at night. It was a dorm room chair for college students, but worked for me and was small enough for Mom to have one too in our shared room. I folded up the chair and neatly placed my blanket on it. I scooted the chair into the corner of the room to give myself a bit of space to get dressed.

I loved my cushion chair bed thing and sharing a room with Mom. I liked being close to her and enjoyed sleeping just a few feet away. She and I stayed up talking, whispering to each other until we fell asleep, like we were at a slumber party or camping. Sometimes she quizzed me, sometimes we dreamed and planned the future.

Our clothes were stored in bins on the floor. I bent to select something for the day, jeans and a sweatshirt, and dug in the bin for some socks and sat back down on the dorm chair to slide them onto my feet. Lori's music oozed out from under her bedroom door as I jumped again over the vent back into the kitchen.

Lori also loved her room. Her teenage years were in full effect, and having her own room was important for everyone. Mom and I gave Lori as much space as possible. Lori's lightly freckled face was natural beauty enough, but she was into makeup now. Her eye liner application around her bright brown eyes every morning took some time, as well as taming her beautiful thick hair to be ready for school. As she emerged from her room, her full lips were pursed and ready with a scathing sarcastic remark or a smirk of satisfaction. The heavy eyeliner did not hide the sadness and anger, quiet and full behind her stare.

Lori was complete and confident with tight fitting jeans, a clean-crisp shirt with the collar popped. Her mornings were mostly on her own, her defiance filtering beneath the door with the sounds of teenage girl preparation and heavy metal music. The donuts were alluring, though, and Lori eventually came out to join us in the new ritual we had begun as a once-again single parent household.

The cozy kitchen, in our doll-size house, was furnished with a single wooden table that we had always had. The table was narrow and small, maybe intended to be a plant stand or placed in front of a window, but it was our kitchen table—well, whenever Mom was single.

The table had grooves in it where the wooden slats had been glued together, and I loved to glide a butter knife down the grooves, digging out the greasy black grime that settled there. There was a dented spot in the middle of the table, from some past damage, which was now worn smooth by touches, and I ran my fingers along the hollow. Smooth and secure, the feeling of the worn wood under my fingertips felt reassuring. The wood had been damaged, but with continued care, it could be made smooth and safe again. There was comfort in knowing the places, knowing the wood, knowing the smell, and fitting my fingers in the scar.

The weak morning light reached through the window over the sink then spilled onto the worn outdoor carpeting glued to the kitchen floor. The oven warmed the tiny space as I waited patiently for the donuts to cook. Twelve minutes to heated gooey dough and flakey sugar goodness.

I leaned against the stove. Mom sat at our little table, her cigarette burning in the ashtray. The coffee cup she lifted to her lips was chipped and stained. The edges of a grin played on her lips as she slurped the dredges of her morning drink. She looked up and smiled at me as she reached forward to prepare her water pipe.

The bong was short, made of translucent purple plastic. Mom wadded up her scrum of pot and crammed it into the small bowl. She glanced up at me to see if I had checked the progress of the donuts. I gave her a nod, still not done, just a few more minutes now.

She flicked the lighter and held her thumb over the small hole in the back of the bong and inhaled. The smoke bubbled through the water. The purple plastic was sticky with brown tar and grime from years of use. The water gurgled, bubbled, and released the thick dense smoke. The smoke coiled up the short distance to her mouth. Mom inhaled deeply, held her breath, emitted a little cough, then held her breath again. Her eyes were glassy; she smiled with a satisfied tight-lipped grin held on her face.

She exhaled, mixing the marijuana scent with the aroma of the baking donuts. In the pause, we made eye contact, acknowledged each other. Mother and daughters, in the warm kitchen, donuts and drugs greeting our morning. Satisfied and accepting.

The donuts came out of the oven, and we let them cool just enough to take a bite. The sweetness coated the back of my throat, and the yeast scent filled the air. The sticky glaze oozed over the warm pastry, clinging to my fingers and leaving white flakes on my lips. I licked the sugar from each finger, gathering each bit of flavor into my mouth.

Mom returned to the bong. Time seemed slow in our frail broken light, the fragrant sugar swirling, co-mingling, and joining the burning marijuana smell. She smoked some more. *Gurgle, inhale, hold, cough, hold.* Her cigarette, left alone, turned to ash. This was breakfast. This was us.

IGLOOS

Our new home was tiny, but there was no Nicoli, no violence, and no random men (yet). It was just Mom, Lori, and me against the world. And I had a new bike as evidence of our fresh start. This was the bike I had been begging for, a bright shiny red ten-speed from Sears.

I was in fifth grade now, and my bike was freedom. I can still feel the crisp morning air stinging my face, my eyes weeping out the sides as I raced through the dark on my new bike on my way to school. Traveling alone before full sunrise, under my own control and direction, affirmed my knowledge of the streets beneath the thin wheels and of my confidence in myself. The early mornings were all part of a greater plan that only now I see.

I rode hard to school every morning, arriving earlier

than most everyone, save the principal. Wound tight and ready to go, I exploded with excessive energy. Mrs. Walsh, the principal, saw me, truly saw me. She watched me arrive in the first light every day and wisely put me to work.

A host of jobs filled those morning hours in the school yard and in the corridors, but most importantly, I raised the flag every morning. Mrs. Walsh impressed upon me the importance of the act, the honor, the service and respect due the flag. Careful to not let it touch the ground, careful to mind the edges, this daily act turned into a moment of mediation, of prayer, of observance. A center point, a focus for my energies, for my attention, I listened to the flapping of the cord against the hollow metallic aluminum pole, the slice of the braided cord rubbing against its neighbor as the flag rose. A reflection and appreciation of the early morning, the time and the honor to raise the flag, became a consistent task that I could control, that I could perform, and that I could count on every day.

My weekly list of assignments included sharpening pencils, straightening offices, and hall monitoring. I would don a yellow and orange vest and work as a guard at the entrance of the school, greeting the stay-at-home moms who dropped their kids off in the parking line, then move inside to monitor the hallways.

These were my assignments, and I took them seriously. I wanted to do well; I wanted to make the principal proud of me. My desire for order and structure became evident at my assigned tasks. These chores created a channel for my energy and began to foster my sense of accountability and responsibility. Mrs. Walsh knew what she what doing, providing an outlet for my energy and time. She did not coddle me; the assignments were important, they were serious, and she counted on me.

Mrs. Walsh and I had been introduced through my earlier trip to her office for fighting on the playground. The fight was a culmination of frustrations, name-calling, and tension fostered by collective friends. I was distanced from it, but allowed myself to be sucked into that energy, people pleasing in a peculiar way.

My foe, Anna, and I had stood across the play yard with our groups of girlfriends around us, egging us on to start something. The kids were eager to see the fight come to physical fruition. Anna had screamed a final insult, which I could not let stand, and the frenzy of the children around me encouraged me to do something about it.

I charged across the brown grass and shoved Anna as hard as I could. She grabbed my hair. That was it. The playground supervisors broke us up. It ended quickly. Recess was over, and we went inside.

About ten minutes into class I heard the firm-heeled footsteps clattering down the hall towards our classroom. I knew who those footsteps were for. Fear clutched my belly. The assistant principal collected Anna and me from class and marched us down the hall to The Office. We sat down in front of the principal's secretary. I am sure that it is intentional, this time to sit in the chairs outside of the principal's office, to prolong the agony and the anxiety. We squirmed in our seats and fielded shameful, knowing glances from teachers and administrators who passed through the office. After what seemed like an hour, Anna and I were ushered into the scary inner sanctum of the principal's office.

Mrs. Walsh sat perched high atop her chair and glared over the top of her glasses, her blond, curly hair bobbing as she asked us what had happened. Anna and I were both embarrassed, crying and attempting to make ourselves small. We curled into our respective seats. We knew this fight was stupid and was not meaningful in any real way to either of us.

We had been goaded by youth, adrenaline, and drama. But here was the evidence that we were different from our drama-filled girlfriends—we had escalated to physical altercation. The principal listened and could see that we were both contrite. Mrs. Walsh said she was going to call our parents, inform them what had happened, then meet with us and our parents separately.

Whew, this was easy for me. I had no emotional response to the statement that she was going to call my mom. I figured it would be difficult for the principal to actually reach my mom. Then it would probably be an extended duration before Mom would carve out time to come to school and sit down with the principal. Finally, and probably most importantly, Mom was never a big fan of authority and the principal's positional power would have little influence on our home life or Mom's opinion of me.

I was not worried about my mom's punishment or disappointment at all. I had gotten off easy. Mom would handle it like a learning opportunity to review with me. Mom received information, processed it at an emotional distance, and moved on. This is how we handled problems.

Wiping my tears away, I glanced over at Anna who had become inconsolable. The news of informing our parents had a much different response from her. She seemed terrified, her tears intensifying to snotty coughing sobs. There was tension in her body as she gripped the arms of her chair. Clearly this punishment meant something else to her.

In my eyes, Anna was the perfect little rich girl. She had everything I had ever wanted. She had two parents at home and lived in a huge house with a pool in the nicest subdivision in town. Anna seemed to have all the stability and order that I craved. She was one of the popular girls and always had a gaggle of friends around her, perfect and cute in their Izods and Polos. She had the perfect clothes, perfectly tanned skin, and perfect petite gymnast body. She was beautiful, with big bright eyes, small nose, and small lips fitted in a heart-shaped face. However, in this moment Anna became real to me. Visible to me. I could see that she was a person and somehow her life was not perfect.

I wondered if she might experience the violence and anger that we had at Nicoli's house. Something in the tension around her mouth, the terror in her eyes, and the hiccupping sobs led both Mrs. Walsh and I to realize that she had something to fear. Anna did not want her parents to be notified; she did not want a meeting with them. Her sobs racked her body, and I was excused so Mrs. Walsh could talk with Anna alone.

Anna and I, over the subsequent years, were never friends, but we were not unfriendly either. At least for me some sort of respect had been borne, in that office, on that playground. We had a shared memory, a brief moment in time, and some kind of unspoken unknown bond.

I had envied her. Then I saw her as a real person with real problems, just like me. Later, during our senior year in high school, Anna moved out of state. The rumors were that she was moving to live with her dad. Her mom and step-dad split up at the same time, and then the step-dad killed himself. The rumors changed about why she moved, something about being sent to a health-care facility for an eating disorder, but we did not move in the same circles, so I really didn't know. But I did know that Anna's life was not perfect.

She was important to me, though, in some inexplicable way. Later someone shared with me the reasons behind her departure senior year. Anna had experienced her own long-term terror, practiced by her step-dad on her, until she finally told her mom. Her mom did not believe her, and she left to live with her dad. She was moving away from her nightmare. Apparently, back then, the long-term abuse was becoming public, so her step-dad shot himself.

I had thought she had everything, but the wealth she was surrounded with did not protect her. Security is not found in wealth unto itself. Although surrounded by all the elements of seeming stability and safety, Anna, too, was on her own path in search of a safe harbor, away from the damage caused by the people entrusted to care for her. She is a beautiful soul, and I continue to be enraptured with her in some way. Little did I know then the commonality we shared.

During this year, in between Mom's men, our times at home were good. Mom and I built a snow fort that winter, we took walks, we gardened together, and meditated on our sticky buns and her bong hits at the table in the morning. But the drug use was back and out in the open. During the Nicoli years, it was greatly reduced and hidden behind the bedroom door. Now the bongs were on the table, the tray at the ready, and the rolling papers handy. Mom figured it was time to teach me to roll a joint.

We did not smoke together, but the ritual, the process was so engaging and a part of my life up until then, so I was curious. Mom was an experiential trainer; she fully believed that you had to experience things for yourself to understand and learn. She taught me to de-stem, de-seed, separate, fluff, and roll a joint. At ten years old, Mom would allow me to twist up her joints and practice this skill. There was no man about to roll them up for her, and that gave us something we could do together. She gave me time and attention, so I loved it. And I admit, the skill did come in handy during my high school years.

Mom typed manuscripts for professors in the evening after work. The tiny living room was furnished with a cherry red love seat that rocked. That love seat was all that could fit into this space. Our thirteen-inch black and white TV sat atop a blanket basket, and at night that would turn into her desk. She would put the TV on the floor and hoist a heavy typewriter onto the basket, pull up the love seat, perch on the edge, and type away.

The clattering, banging safe sounds of the typewriter

reassured me that she was there, she was working and sober. She typed fast, her hands always moving. As a young child, she was taught to play piano. She would play for her mom when we went to visit her parents. She could bang out the most powerful and moving song on the piano, "The Headless Horseman," and I begged her to play it every time. I was thrilled at her ability to make music with her hands. To this day, when Mom hugs me or holds my hand, she plays. Her fingers move constantly, playing an imaginary piano or typing out a book. Her fingers press into my flesh with a reassuring melody of movement. Back then, the notes made my pulse race, and I was fast riding along the dark muddy path with the headless horsemen in the lead.

Mom was running too, running from her third failed marriage and her unwanted childhood. Her mother had never fully accepted her. Her parents had not wanted another child so late in life, and my mom was a surprise, a full ten years younger than her sister. My mother's mom had her own brand of violence, laced with dismissal and disdain. Mom was routinely sent off to her aunt or her sister's house after a violent episode at the hands of her mother.

Grandma Marie was deeply unhappy. Pregnant

with Lori at age sixteen, Mom got married and moved into student housing with Lori's dad. Her indoctrination into the university campus at such a young age at that time in the late sixties led to the hippie drug addict life that engulfed her. Grandma never forgave her, never allowed her to be who she was, and did not love her unconditionally until after the death of Mom's dad.

Mom was close to her dad, Tom. He had taught her to fish, to garden, to recognize plants. She was his confidant, his joy, and his little buddy. It could be surmised that Grandma disliked Mom because of her relationship with Grandpa, but really the scars were deeper than that.

Once a year, we would visit Tom and Marie's home, a wild country place with sprawling acres, coal pits, and sunshine. Grandma's property was friendly with gardens, bee hives, and fruit orchards. The summer visits were fine, gorgeous days, filled with chores and exploring, weeding the garden, strawberries and beans, chasing snakes, spying spiders, and feeding peanuts to the chickens. We picked apples, peeled them, and baked them into scrumptious cobblers. We would stay overnight, sleeping in the guest room on the double bed, crisp clean cotton sheets with the perfect pillows and smooth quilted bedspread.

Grandma would retire early, talking on her CB as the "Chigger Lady" and sleeping on a plastic couch. That summer I visited all by myself for the first time. Every night I begged Grandma to let me sleep with her on the burnt orange plastic couch. I wanted to be snuggled, and feel safe next to her, and listen to her scratchy voice as she exchanged with the strangers on the radio. The dial lit the living room, casting a shadow across our faces.

She did not relent. I was to sleep in the guest bed, alone with the country sounds. On the final night of my visit, I was invited to sleep with my grandpa. I was happy to have a partner, but the way in which Grandma informed me gave me pause and made me nervous. Grandma reminded me that I did not have to sleep with Grandpa if I did not want to. She also reminded me that at any time if I got scared, I could come out and sleep in the guest room. She was clear: I could not join her on the couch, but if I wanted, I could sleep in the guest room.

These warnings seemed ominous. Was I an offering? Was it supposed to be my choice? Was I supposed to know to not sleep with him? Her eyes gave warning, but she said nothing more, and my grandpa's arms seemed reassuring enough and we settled in. Quickly, I realized an error, as uncomfortable antsy feelings gripped me. It was not peaceful or safe; it felt scary and intimidating in the dark with him. I held out hope that I was imagining things and the night would pass without incident.

"Hope, why don't you snuggle next to me?" Grandpa cooed.

"Ummmm, I am comfortable over here," I stammered.

"Oh, don't be scared, I won't hurt you. Besides didn't you want to sleep in here with me? Just come snuggle up," he stated simply.

I remained motionless, too scared to move, too scared to leave, paralyzed in the moment. My young intuition was in full warning mode, and fear seized my movements. He reached over and pulled me near. It was not a snuggle, not the safe comforting spooning that parents and children enjoy; it was more of a forced slide. He slid my body next to his.

I remained stiff and flat on my back, afraid, and hoping the fear would pass. He reached down and slid his hands into my pajamas. I closed my eyes, squeezed back tears, and held my breath. His fingers fiddled with my labia, my little girl vagina. He was probing his fingers into my spaces. I started shaking, my lip quivered from fear. I remained motionless and silent.

He pushed down my jammies and panties. He bent over me, his mouth found my privates. Wet and probing, licking and urging. I started to feel sick, the swallow of puke bubbled up my throat.

I was paralyzed. My mind racing, freezing, blood flooded my face, heart pounded, but I was unable to move, breathe, or speak. He must have felt my tension. I did not move against his urging mouth. He relented and retreated. He unfolded himself from being bent over me. Silent tears rolled down the sides of my face. I remained frozen to my spot. He grabbed my hand and placed it on his semi-hard penis.

"Can you feel that?" he asked. "Can you feel how happy you have made me?"

I held in the puke, the fear, and open sobbing. I held my breath. I did not move my hand in any way.

"Do you want to touch it?" he asked. "Mmmm, it feels good when you touch me there."

I wanted to scream for my mom, but I knew she

wasn't there. I lay there wishing I would wake up from this bad dream.

He moved my hand up and down, beginning to rub himself to a firmer hardness. The fear ballooned in my mind like a blinding spot. The black spot grew, narrowing out the light and closing in on my senses. I felt dizzy. I thought I would throw up.

"Why don't you put it in your mouth?" He hummed. His sweet voice was sickening. "Don't you want to make me feel good?"

This thought broke me. I started to whimper and uttered the smallest, "No, I can't." Those were all the words I could muster. "I don't want to. I'm afraid," I apologized.

"Come on, Hope, it won't hurt, I promise I won't hurt you." He stated like it was the most straightforward thing in the world, like he had stated it before, like he did not know the terror behind my clinched eyes. "I won't put it in you, if you just put it in your mouth, we can do it that way." He paused, waiting for my response. He continued to urge my hand up and down.

The room was soft dark, the powder blue walls seemed to close in on me, but from somewhere I gathered the strength, I gathered the pieces of myself to resist. "I can't, I just can't." Saying the statements out loud created a physical strength and courage that, up until now, had fled my mind and body. I began to pull back, to take myself back.

I pulled my hand away, scooted up my panties and my jammies. I slunk out of the bed, careful to leave the blankets undisturbed to keep everything hidden under the thin white bed cover. I did not want to see. I shuffled out of the room.

In the hall, I began to cry softly, the fear rolling off of me with the tears. My grandma came and ushered me into the guest room, a mere twelve feet from my grandpa's bedroom. She asked what was wrong, but she knew. She knew because she had warned me with her eyes. This was not the first time she had ushered one of her granddaughters out of her husband's room crying in the night. She may have not known exactly what occurred, but the girls experienced something frightful in that room.

"I just feel sick," I told her. "I think I have a tummy ache and I don't want to bother Grandpa. I might throw up," I stated, which was true. After hiding in the bathroom for a bit, I emerged. Thankfully, she had waited for me outside the bathroom door. She tucked me into the guest bed, the cold sheets dry against my skin. She left me alone there to wonder, to let my fear ebb and flow. Would he come in there? Would he ask for an explanation? Would he force me to do more?

The guest room felt safer, if only because I was alone in a bed, but not safer because I did not know what else might happen. I was wide awake afraid in that room, listening to the sounds of the country and the opening of grandpa's bedroom door. I edged myself to the furthest lip of the bed, furthest from the door, and readied myself for any entrance to the room, but that never came, and eventually I fell into a fitful sleep.

Mom arrived the next day to take me home. She spent the day visiting with her parents, oblivious to the pain I had experienced. I was sullen, moody, in hopes that my bad behavior would initiate questioning. None came. No questions arose, and I did not tell.

As we drove away in our blue Volkswagen Rabbit with the black plastic seats, I looked out the back window and stared at their house. We bumbled down the gravel road, and I looked back at that house and knew something had happened that changed me, which would mark me, and that made me different than I had been before. I was now a stranger in my own mind; I was in third person looking from behind myself at the back of my head staring out the window at the sad, angry house. I was different.

Grandma held onto her anger, and she and my mom's relationship remained strained until the death of Grandpa. After he died, Marie became happy, pleasant to be around, and genuinely herself. She then bestowed unto Mom the unconditional love that she had withheld all those years. Mom did not know the evil that had lurked behind her dad's mind, and she still struggles today with the things that were revealed and discovered after his death. However, he remains what he was to her, her memories intact and her body left unexplored by his hands.

As it should be, their relationship was theirs, was what it was, and the discoveries later in life do not change her childhood or young adulthood and her knowledge of him. She believed he loved her in the purest way, in a way he might not have loved anyone. However, it is curious if her relationship was as happy and untainted as she portrays, what is her struggle with men? Why the cycle of men in her life?

Today mom is three years sober and in her seventh marriage; maybe she has found what she has been searching for.

MICROBIOLOGY

J oy pops her head into the laboratory. "Hope, do you have a second?"

"Of course." I turn from my computer and look up at her. "What's up?"

"Can you come down to my office?"

I lock my computer screen and head down the hall to her cozy office. Joy is my boss's boss, but her office is pretty small, yet simple, orderly and functional.

"Have a seat." Joy settles into her chair behind the desk. She has a sign posted on the wall: *Bad Systems will defeat Good People every time.*

I sit in the chair across from her and give a small smile, little shrug, and raised eyebrows. "Do you need something?"

"I was wondering what your plans were?" she asks, smiling.

"My plans?" I scrunch up my face in a quizzical look and tilt my head.

"Yes, your plans for your career."

"Oh." I pause. "Well, I mean, I've been here for just over a year. I'm getting along with the group. I guess I have not thought much about it." I realize as I say this, it is probably all the wrong answer, but it's the truth. I was in my third company since graduating from college, and so far, I had made the job changes to earn more money.

"Well, I think we should start thinking about that." Her brown eyes are soft but direct.

I nod and say nothing.

"You have a natural skill set. You have leadership capabilities," Joy continues. "The team here is very tenured, as you know," her eyes conveying all the background information that I was fully aware of.

"You are younger than the least-oldest by ten years. They have all been here for ten to twenty years, and they all like you and have taken to your guidance. I know you do not have HR responsibilities for them, but you do all of their scheduling and coordination of lab work and sample collection." She pauses for my reaction.

"Yeah," I stumble. "My first boss out of college told me about *Seven Habits of Highly Effective People*, and that I should make deposits into relationships before making withdrawals. That analogy really works for me, and I have tried to do that with the team." I pause, but then plow on. "I have collected samples, gotten gowning qualified, and came in on holidays to rotate the plates. I mean, I want to do my share. Even if I am scheduling all of the work and sort of directing our activities." My voice trails off, not knowing where I am going with this.

"I know, it is all great. We are impressed with what you have been able to do."

I stare at her expectantly.

Joy smiles. "We might be looking for a supervisor soon, and I wanted to discuss your interest and readiness."

My eyes widened. "Yes, of course. Thank you," I blurt out, clearly not ready, but excited about new challenges and opportunities.

"Why don't we start at the career development center?" Joy hands me a slip of paper with a name and email address on it. "This is Coreen; she will help get you started."

With that, my career, or at least my career planning, began to take shape. The Eli Lilly career development center started out by having me take a strengths assessment and an interest assessment. The interest assessment was crucial for me because my interests were so varying and I had no real direction of what I wanted to do. They set me up with mentors, and I shadowed different departments and people to help build a plan.

Up until that point, I had made job moves simply to increase my salary. When one of my colleagues left the microbiology lab we were working in to go to Lilly, I gave her my resume and told her to let me know if a position opened up. A few months later, she said there was a job I should apply for and she would refer me. It was in an Environmental Monitoring lab, which was a portion of what I did in the microbiology lab already, so I applied and got the position.

After working with the Lilly career development center, I began to be able to verbalize my skill set and recognize my strengths. I looked to take on positions of increasing authority and responsibility. I learned three important things, well much more, while I worked at Eli Lilly, but three important things that I have carried with me ever since.

The first of which is the career planning that Coreen got me started on. The tool set I used then has morphed over time, and I have crafted it to my own framework that I now use with many employees and mentees. However, the focus, the goals setting, the planning, and the core of the material initiated from that first conversation I had with Joy.

Another important lesson was an understanding of my own capacity for work. I love the challenge. This was the time in my life that I started working ten-to-twelve-hour days. I loved it. Being stretched intellectually, learning new regulations and requirements all the time, coordinating complex projects and facility-wide qualifications in partnerships with operations, quality, engineers, and facilities personnel was awesome. I coordinated the schedule for nine people, ran the laboratory, and ensured our activities were completed on time. I soaked up the stimulation. I wanted to work hard. I wanted to push the boundaries of my own capabilities.

This amount of work and capacity for work led me to another learning, which is vital for career growth too: when and how to say no and manage up. At one point, I had seventeen different qualifications in various stages of completion. These qualifications were complex to compile, and can be explained as three phases: compilation and planning, sample collection and execution, closure and implementation. They were all in various stages, and a few needed closer oversight and problem-solving. Although I did not want to, I took three of the qualifications to my boss and asked her to give them to someone else to oversee the execution. They were already built and ready to go; they just needed to launch.

In order to do my job well, I had to be comfortable handing off some of the workload so I could execute my responsibilities properly. The lab, the department, and ultimately our patients would be better served if I asked for help. This is an important lesson in managing workload, managing up, and prioritizing activities.

All of these lessons were started with that visit with Joy, and yet I still have more to learn.

NORTH WOODLAWN

I loved the times when we had a men-free home, and we enjoyed that for an entire year. Then we moved again. Mom had secured us another tiny bungalow. The weekend we moved in, Mom and I painted the entire house. I remember the effort, the fun of it, setting our goal to complete it in one day, and staying focused until the task was completed. After thirteen hours, every room was painted, a new color for us—antique white—and we rested in the empty living room, sitting on the floor, drinking tap water and eating whole wheat and Muenster cheese sandwiches. We were getting the new home off on the right foot. It felt good, and I thought Mom might be able to stay in this new chapter of living.

Mom's office manager job at the dentist office did not earn enough money, though, so she took a second job waitressing at night. At first, this seemed like a boon, but soon the draw of the nightlife returned us to the old ways. Unpredictability began to be our norm again. The brief respite of boyfriend-free life, respectable work, and sobriety faded away. The bar was a source of solid income for Mom. She made more money there than at the dentist office, one of her many recent jobs in this time period, but it put her back in the environment that spoke to her inner demons and addictions. The bar became a source once again for endless drugs, alcohol, and sex partners.

Lori had her own room in this house, while Mom and I shared. Our room was different; it was a bedroom in which a loft had been built. Oak hardwood steps lifted you to the loft that was large enough for a built-in bed platform and a bookshelf. The loft was open to the room below, where my twin bed sat. We had found an oak desk in the college students' trash, stripped it of its antique green paint, and it became my dresser, desk, and work station. I loved the sturdiness of that desk from the trash, and I kept it into my early thirties.

Along with the alcohol and drug use ratcheting up, mom began the cycle of men through the house. Waking up to mom having sex with a stranger was becoming more and more frequent. The sex sessions were extra loud for me now because I shared the room with her. It was always the same, stirring awake to the urging, hunger sounds of the adults in the loft above my head. I would hold my breath and wait. The smell of sex wafted down the stairs, the sweat, and the sweet smell of pot lingered too.

This was the soundtrack (and smell-track) of my life. The cycle, the churn. The men were unknown to me; occasionally one would rise up to the level of introduction, but rarely did they become boyfriends. Who were these men? How had it been to sneak past the bed of a sleeping child to venture up to a loft to have sex? Did my sleeping form do nothing to squelch the desire? Did they not have anywhere else to go? Or were they too drugged out to notice?

The drugs, the alcohol, and the parade of men was the onset of an even deeper level of addiction for Mom. The brief time of attentiveness had passed, and it was no longer us against the world; it was each one of us for ourselves. Mom was on the search for the next boyfriend, husband, or distraction, and the search led her to settle on a drug dealer, Jacob.

Jacob was the ultimate in cool: tall and lean, dark

sunglasses, long hair, played lead guitar in a band, and wore tight black leather pants that showed off his ass. He could expertly roll a joint and pretended to be an intellectual, like all pot smokers.

Jacob drove a 1971 Lincoln Town Car, still with its original white paint job, gleaming black leather top, and suicide doors. The leather interior was starting to wear and tear, but it was a badass car with its huge dials on the dash, stick to put into drive, and the silver manual radio buttons. It smelled like an old car, and of course the marijuana fumes had permeated the leather too. We would coast around in that boat of a car, Jacob and Mom and me all in the front seat, listening to Bob Marley, with their pot smoke billowing out the windows.

Mom's relationship with Jacob marked the final demise of our already fractured girl trio of together-ness. Lori would not play along. Lori had had her own battle with a man named Jacob, and Mom had let her lose. Lori was simply done with being nice to Mom's men-of-the-hour.

Lori's teen rage was fully formed, and she was battling her own social inequities at the public high school. We were on the lower end of the socio-economic scale, and the popular kids at school made no effort to blunt the pain of that inequity. We knew where we stood, and our drug addict, alcoholic, single mother was common knowledge too.

We were guilty by association. Lori struggled in school, both academically and socially. She began her own trip down alcohol lane and, after some life-altering social decisions, her anger had nowhere to go, except directed at Mom and me.

She lashed out. Violence exploded regularly in our bungalow home du jour. Property and objects were routinely destroyed. Lori raged around while Mom was out of the house venting her frustration at life on me. She would chase me into my room, and even if I could latch the eye-hook lock quickly enough, she would not relent, pounding on the door and hissing at me. She threatened to kick the door down, and one day she did.

It was terrifying, looking into the eyes of my sister, who had just kicked the bedroom door off its hinges. Afraid of the blows that would soon pummel me, I cowered in the corner of my room, but Lori was too stunned to come after me and continue the fight. She was surprised that the door had crumpled under her heel, and we both stood for a moment in silence. We then became partners in repair. We had to fix the door before Mom got home. It became a pattern. Lori would rage, I would run, and Lori would actively destroy something to the point of joint terror.

In the fallout we became partners, partners to fool Mom, partners to cover up the damage. Once we had to repaint my bedroom. We rearranged furniture to hide destruction in the walls, and fixed tables and chairs to usable conditions all before Mom got home. We would sweep up, mop up, and clean the blood off my face in order to prevent Mom from finding out the extent of the violence experienced that day.

As bad as it was, Lori's supreme rage was saved for the big exchanges with Mom. We each had long ago learned to embrace our roles: Lori the disrupter, Mom the neglecter, and I the peacemaker. My peacekeeper role was important in this home, and I honed my skills here. They both accepted my role, which allowed me to send them to their corners and be the calm in the center of the emotional storm.

However, the anger and the outbursts increased in intensity, with both strength and weaponry. The fighting became too frequent. Lori was relentless in letting Mom know how awful she was, what a terrible parent she was, and how Lori hated her in the deepest marrow of her being. They embarked on a series of fights that no peacekeeping measures could stay and culminated one hot summer evening.

This event began over the trifle of our lives, and is lost to all reasons that fights start, but Lori was ready to raise the bidding in this war. The warm evening may have escalated tempers more quickly, as the muggy air hung heavy. The dark night seeped into the edges of their hearts and neither would allow the other room for reprieve or safety. The shouting ensued, and the insults hurled. Their yelling thronged in the air with crashing plates and glassware and upturned furniture.

Weapons were chosen hastily. Lori picked up the orange cut glass of a broken plate and threw it too near Mom's head. Mom retaliated with shoving the small kitchen table over onto Lori. Lori returned by throwing a kitchen chair at her. They gave chase into the living room, but that was bare, we had no furniture in there, so hand-to-hand combat ensued. I stood by, wailing at them to stop, but my screams bounced off the noise bellowing from their throats. Shoves, hair pulling, open-hand slapping, and closed fists were exchanged. They were a scrappy, gangly mess of sweat, screams, and deep sadness.

Extracting herself from the fray, Lori lunged into the kitchen to pilfer a knife. She grabbed a wooden-handled serrated knife. She glared at Mom, and I feared the worst, but instead of diving at Mom, she ran out the front door. Mom ran after her. With a thrust and a pounce, Mom grabbed Lori's arm and wrested the knife from her gripping hand. With a hard shove at Mom, Lori took off towards the railroad track. Mom chased after her with the rusted blade in hand. Lori's sixteen-year-old legs outpaced Mom as she disappeared into the inky night.

I watched from the porch, huffing, sucking air, out of breath from screaming and crying. I had watched the whole scene in disbelief. Lori's rage was not new; it was common and known. But Mom could typically dial back her anger. This night she did not.

Mom usually held her feelings at bay and let Lori move through hers. Not on this night; Mom had gone to the dark side. Mom's anger blinded her to the daughter before her. This night marked a turning point. Our home was untenable. In our sane moments we knew this. Now it was out in the open. For Mom and Lori to stay under the same roof would only spell inevitable and irreversible harm. They both could no longer trust themselves.

Lori, at the age of sixteen, moved into her own place, a musty basement apartment, and down her own destructive path. Unfettered by parental involvement, although the skills certainly had been learned at home, her battle was now her own.

And Mom and I moved again.

ROLL OUT

What is that? I look closer and see our living room window opening. The window is being lifted from inside, as we coast up the driveway. A body folds over and tuck-n-rolls out the window.

A toned, tanned skin man with long blond hair drops to his feet, catches a glance at our car pulling into the driveway, and bolts toward the front yard. White plastic bag in hand, he flits behind the bushes.

Jacob slams the Lincoln into park, jerking the car to a stop. The thief starts up the tree-covered hill heading to the street above our dead-end home.

Jacob and I throw open our doors, while the car is still stopping. I move automatically, no thought, just move. Flight.

Run. Catch. Move. Chase. Mom sits in the middle of the front bench seat. Jacob and I race.

We are close behind, the thief's footsteps leading the way. A second man appears in the woods, right before my eyes. He turns to run behind the first guy. Now we are after two of them.

We crest into the street above the woods. I am in pursuit of the second guy and Jacob in pursuit of the first one. The second thief peels away and heads west at the first intersection. Without discussion, without voice, Jacob and I focus on the blond. He is the one with the bag. He is the one who rolled out of the window.

He is a grown man, but we are running him down to get back whatever is in the bag. We are within twenty yards, he is far enough away that we can't grab him, but we are within running reach. The chase spills east into the neighborhood streets.

Jacob is yelling at the man. I do not hear his words. They remain unformed in my mind. I am focused, clear, and breathing hard. I am pushing my lithe thirteen-year-old body as fast as I can to aid Jacob, and protect my home. I am pacing, moving with hands straight, tall body and long strides.

I want to catch him, Eric; I know who the thief is. I want to snatch him, rip the bag of drugs from his hands, and thrust the bag back to Jacob, triumphant. I love to run. I love feeling my strong body move against the concrete and push forward to be ever faster. I love having a focus, a goal. The race of adrenaline, fear, and excitement courses through me and propels my steps to equal the grown men I am racing with.

The thief cuts into the backyard between two houses, and at first Jacob and I are running side-by-side, but we split up down either side of the block. Eric races between the houses, Jacob and I cover him from both sides. I catch snatches of his racing-form steps ahead of us, but now thirty yards to the side. I see Jacob on the other side of the houses on the next block over. His thin long brown hair and dark sunglasses glinting past the 1960s ranch homes.

Then he is gone. Eric disappeared. One house passed too many. *Is he hiding? Is he bunkered down in a dog house? Is he backtracking and now going in the opposite direction?*

The race slows as the rabbit is no longer visible to the greyhounds, we have nothing to chase. We need to collect ourselves and search. Eric has the drugs. He has the bag, and he must be close.

He was only thirty yards away at last glimpse, and

he was in between Jacob and I. We start retracing our steps at a light jog. Peering down between the houses, *Where is this guy?* Jacob is still on the other side; he is backtracking too. As the block ends, we come together. We realize our quarry has slipped our grip.

As my heart rate eases, then my mind starts to ponder. *Exactly what was I thinking?* Without thought or conscience decision, I had thrown open the car door and raced after a grown man. In my blind of adrenaline, my immediate reaction was to give chase. We race. I am a thirteen-year-old girl, fully formed, but no match for a grown man. I could not out-power Eric. *What was I going to do if I caught him?* These thoughts did not enter my mind until I slowed to a walk.

Jacob puts his arm around my shoulders, both of us are breathing hard. We are disappointed that we did not catch him. Jacob is not too worried because he knows who it was, and a smirky smile plays on his face. I stupidly ask if we are going to call the police, but then quickly dismiss my own question as it dissolves in my mouth. You don't call the police when your stash is stolen. I wonder what drugs or small amount of cash, or both, was in the white plastic bag.

I know Jacob deals drugs, but I am not sure in what

quantities, and not always sure it is limited to marijuana. Eric is what was considered a "family friend," one of the many guys who hung around. They are always buying something, selling something, getting stoned, drunk or both. The male harem of hangers on, mooching off of the primary stash, drinking the house booze, and eyeing the teenage girls. The churn of men had started and would only grow.

DEAD END

My friend situation was fluid and changed with each move and each new school. Mom never sent me to a public kindergarten. I went straight into first grade, and by the next year we had a moved a few times, and I was in another school for second grade and so it went.

The constant moving forced me to develop a fast-friends approach. On the first day at a new school, I picked out people who seemed nice, and I acted like their best friend. I certainly was not aware that this was my "method," but upon reflection I see this approach. It worked in grade school, but as I got into my pre-teens this practice was received with less and less acceptance.

When Mom and her latest boyfriend Jacob decided to live together, instead of him moving in with us in the bungalow, Mom moved us into his dumpy brick duplex on the bad side of town where addicts went to score, complete with a dirt patch yard and a dog chained in front.

Thankfully, we were only there for a few short weeks. Jacob had just painted my room purple, and the next day we were evicted. I was old enough to know what this meant and to be embarrassed. I was once again unsure of our next landing spot. It was only a few days of living in the car.

They moved us into a dead-end home, both literally and figuratively, on the other side of town, in a decent neighborhood, but into which our crappy house was nestled. I was in eighth grade now and, in order to not change schools again, I walked a mile to a bus stop that took me to my old school.

I found the walk sublime. Chilly mornings, dark and alone, listening on my Walkman to Bon Jovi's "Living on a Prayer" made me feel free and somehow powerful. The opening sounds of that song and leaves rustling in the wind still bring me back to those early morning walks.

That daily walk edged me on the boarder of the university campus, past dormitories, record stores, head shops, and college housing with stained couches on the front porch. The bus would ramble up and collect my lone figure in the cloak of the grey skies, my head clear and focused on the school day ahead with the Walkman cranked up full blast to block out my inner thoughts and worries.

After a few months of making this morning trek, Bon Jovi and me, I changed my mind and decided that I would go to the school in my district. I figured I would be going to high school with the people at the closer school, so I should probably attempt to find some fast-friends before then.

When I showed up as the new girl six weeks before the end of the school year, I was instantly reunited with one of the commune kids, Katy. Katy's parents had straightened up their wayward youths and were successful business people now, but Katy knew me. She had always known me. We were intrinsic souls meant to spend time together in this lifetime.

I used my fast-friend technique on a group of established girls at the school. I joined them at lunch, talked to them incessantly and just acted like I was part of their group. Two girls, Susan and Nicole, had known each other since kindergarten going to the same schools, lived close to each other, and here I was showing up, oblivious, acting like I had been there with them all along. I joined in and they did not push me out, so I stayed. I learned later that they hated me those first weeks and had no idea who I was or what I was doing acting like their best friend.

Susan became a dear friend. She was a sweet, down-home girl, raised in a happy, stable two-parent home. The first time I spent the night there I was instantly aware of the stability and comfort the home held. Susan's parents drank beer socially, and her older brother might have dabbled in drugs, but when I came into her life she was introduced to the dark underbelly of drugs and addiction found at my house.

The first time she was to spend the night with me, Jacob rolled up in his '71 white Lincoln Town Car to pick us up. Susan took in the scene, that big car, Jacob with his sunglasses reflecting in the sun, and his black-red-yellow-and-green Jamaican tam sloped back on his head. She shot me a look but said nothing. We loaded up, both Susan and I sitting in the front. I was in the middle and could feel her body tense up.

She was entering into a foreign world. Her parents both drove sensible Fords, well taken care of by her father. Here she was now with this long-haired man, a

1971 car, and both of us sitting in the front bench seat so friendly and cozy. I saw the moment of consideration on her face as she clenched the door handle and read her thoughts. Was she safe? Should she get in the car with this man? She took a deep breath and pulled the suicide door shut.

She did not know the ride she would be taking with me, my sweet Susan. Although she was hesitant to get in that car, something in her gut must have trusted me. We coasted out of the parking lot, and Jacob turned on his reggae music, leaned over, and pushed in the cigarette lighter. He fished a joint from behind his ear.

The car lighter popped and Jacob reached for it, nodding his head along with the rhythm of the music. The whole movement was dismissed by me, this was my life. Susan watched with wide eyes as Jacob poked the joint in his mouth, pressing the lighter coils to singe the end. He puffed a few times to get it properly lit, then deeply inhaled and held his breath. Susan held her breath too and stole a look at me from the corner of her eye. "One love, one light, let's get together and feel alright …" Marley crooned to us.

Susan grabbed my elbow and stared at me. Her eyes were questioning, darting sideways towards Jacob and the joint. I can only imagine what this was like for her. She had never been around drugs, she had never heard reggae music, and she had probably never even been in a car with a man with long hair. I looked at her. *What?* I asked with my eyes and a head tilt. She widened her already saucer eyes, pressed her lips tight together. I shrugged. I put my hand on hers, which was still gripping my elbow, and turned to face forward again. Jacob hummed to us "How was school today, girls?"

I chattered on, but Susan just looked straight ahead and hung on. We lived in a broken-down house on a dead-end street. The reason Jacob and Mom wanted this house was because of the woods in the front yard and there were no neighbors. The dead-end gravel road ended in a sort of bowl at the bottom of a bigger road. There was another house in the gravel bowl with us, but it was uninhabited. Mom waxed poetic talking about the house when first explaining it to me. "Oh, Hopey, you will love it! You have to pass under a bush to get to the porch."

This was true, but it was not designed that way, it was because the nature elements grew unchecked. The house was actually condemned and deemed uninhabitable, but the owners were happy to rent it to us anyway. I figured anything was better than sleeping in the car.

The house had a partial dirt basement, and the beams were eaten up by termites. The only source of heat was a wood stove. Lessons in heating with wood are valuable. Starting a fire, waking in the night to re-stoke it, managing household heat could be used for post-apocalyptic living if needed. I feel prepared.

My room was a back porch, where the winter windows had been left in place. The roof sagged dangerously from the termite damage and from improper construction. The back-porch room was adjacent to the tiny, freezing bathroom that held all the same peculiarities. The bathtub was ringed with dark mold and ever threatened to fall through the floor boards. An MC Escher mirror ball poster hung in the bathroom, staring back at you from inside his distant and twisted mind, quietly reminding you of where you were.

But it was my room, and I was happy to have it. I had started cleaning my own room at ten years old, making sure my space was orderly and clean. Here at our latest house, this became a more concerted effort. The remainder of the house was in shambles and disorder, but my room was well kept. I kept my trash-found rug clean and made my bed every day. The fact that my bed was a mattress on the floor did not matter. My clothes were hung up and color coded. I had tons of drawings, pictures and posters on the walls. Mom and Jacob allowed me to paint my door, which had a Plexiglass window that covered the top portion. I painted giant circles on it with random colors that we had around the house. I had a growing desire to expand a sense of order to the remainder of the hovel we called home.

More than once during the years there, I had Mom call me in sick from school so I could stay home to clean the house. I bleached the kitchen. Every inch, every corner of that sticky, grimy, kitchen was scrubbed. I emptied all of the cabinets, wiped them down, and replaced all the items in an organized manner. The bleach burned my hands, but I didn't care. Unfortunately, the condition of the home made it feel like it was never clean. The stained kitchen floor, the broken cabinets, the furring-strips and plaster walls were warped and misshapen, so even when clean, the house was incongruent in some way.

The wood stove was effective at keeping the small

house warm, except my back-porch bedroom and the ice-cold bathroom, but it also kept the house full of dust and soot. The best I could do was to keep my room in order and fight back the madness in the rest of the house when I could.

It was a big deal to bring a new friend here. Susan was someone of wealth (I believed) and stability. To share my mattress on the floor, the trash collected furniture, this meant something. Like most things, I charged forward with abandon, not letting the fear or insecurities catch up with me. Susan had already proven we were friends, and I did not give much thought to if she would reject me now, because of my home. It would have been acceptable and understandable if, after that first visit—starting with the pot-choked car and then sleeping on my seedy mattress—she de-friended me. But she didn't. Susan never gave any indication of hesitation again, after the first moments in the Lincoln. She seemed to accept the environment and was along for the ride. I always wondered what her parents must have thought when they first picked her up at my house, but our friendship remained steadfast.

Susan had grown up in the sticks, the nearest house to hers was about a mile away. She had never been downtown and was not accustomed to walking miles to get anywhere like we did. Katy and I showed her a new way to live. We walked all over the university campus and downtown and rode city buses. Those first few walks, Susan was afraid the whole time. We walked past frat houses with beer pong on the front porches, hot guys standing outside howling at us as we passed. Katy and I were fearless (the stupidity of youth). We would yell back taunting sweet nothings to these young men several years older than us. We encouraged Susan to keep up. We gleefully instructed: "Just keep walking." "We are fine." "They won't bother us."

Although Katy's parents were not on the same path they had been "back in the day," and I had lost touch with her throughout the years, she and I instantly reconnected. Katy had enjoyed stability, living with her parents in the same house, and went to the same primary school for the duration of her formative years. Katy and I were born two days apart, and our mothers were in the same hospital at the same time; maybe this is where our bond was formed. We were close through the early years on the commune and then off and on we would get together for play dates.

During the Nicoli era, we lived on the south side

of town, only three miles from Katy's house. I rode my bike, when I was six or seven years old, to her house across town. I still remember her phone number 336-2780. I would call her, and she would answer, "Is Katy there?" to leave me sputtering and confused, as these were the days before caller ID. So naturally when I showed up at her middle school, I immediately had a friend. I did not have to use my fast-friend technique on her. She already knew my dark home. Addiction and alcoholism had spent time in her home as well; it had passed but she knew its ravages.

Mom was now a waitress at a place called Nick's. She worked nights in the dim, smoky bar where the employees started drinking midway through their shift. Nick's was the oldest restaurant and tavern in town with history and tradition, and many of the employees had degrees, but delayed, or never, got career jobs. The bar industry is fraught with people fighting their own addictions. Mom had moved us out of the commune, but now she essentially worked at one.

Many of the same principles applied. Alcohol was alarmingly consumed, pot was smoked, cocaine lines were snorted, and pills were popped, with everyone exchanging lovers as needed. Pseudo-intellectuals, these "smart" degreed folks were blurring their minds with drugs. The line between our house and the bar was blurry too. It was common for after-parties to spontaneously form at our house after the crew got off work. After all, Jacob was their drug dealer. He kept the Nick's team supplied with pot and coke, and could get the other goods as needed and upon request. There seemed an endless stream of drunken men and women traipsing through the house.

At least I had a door to my back-porch room. Mom rarely got home before three or four in the morning. She would laugh loud and hiccup as she stumbled through the house. The slanting, tilting floor and her drunken state were a bad mix; hard falls routinely shuddered the rickety house. Most nights, I would briefly wake up, listen to make sure she did not hurt herself and had at least made it to her bed, then I would allow myself to go back to sleep before my 6:00 a.m. alarm sounded to arise and get myself to school.

Our house was the party house, and annually the Nick's crew held a pig roast there. They would dig a pit in the front yard and bury a pig in the pit to cook. This was a three-day alcohol and fuck fest. Alcohol was everywhere, drugs were everywhere, and the house was full of thirty-somethings and forty-year-olds partying like rock stars. People passed out on the mattresses in the living room coined "day beds," in tents on the lawn, and laid out flat on the gravel driveway.

They had stashes of alcohol and pot everywhere, and it was one of these weekends that Katy and I decided it was time for us to join the party.

GTO

Katy and I took a bottle of white liquor out of Mom's sewing machine drawer.

Why was a bottle of white liquor stashed in Mom's sewing machine drawer? Why did we snatch it? I have no idea; my world had no order or reasoning.

Katy and I took the bottle and walked out of the house with the booze in a paper bag. No one, of course, noticed.

We walked in the general direction toward campus, taking turns swigging from the bottle, and ended up at our favorite bathroom in the student union. The bathroom had pink settee seats and mirrors that came together in the corners. In these mirrors you could see yourself repeated forever. We polished off the bottle, which must not have been full to start with, or else we might have died drinking a half gallon of straight liquor for our first taste of alcohol.

Katy and I stared at ourselves in the abyss of those mirrors, wondering aloud of the impossibility of it, delving into our own false pseudo-intellectualism. What if these were representative of alternate universes or realms? Is that just us reflected in another space and time? Giggling and hoping that no one would catch us, the mirrors giggled back and told us we were all right. We stumbled and bumbled our way to sit on a wall on the edge of campus. We watched cars cruising around the small town "loop."

Sitting on the wall, blind drunk, we cat-called boys driving by in muscle cars. Two boys stopped (which is what we had been hoping for). These boys were cute and country. Katy scooted into the back, and I plopped into the front seat.

"How y'all doin'?" the freckle-faced, sloppy brown-haired driver asked with a half-smile.

"Pretty good," we slurred in response.

"Where y'all want to go?" our driver asked.

"How fast does this thing go?" I smiled at him in my drunken attempt to be coy.

"We've gotten her up to 120 miles per hour before."

"No way! I don't believe it!" I grinned.

"Let's prove it!"

We made our way to Highway 37, where he opened up the engine and we screamed through the night. Stupid drunken youth, free in the dark night, no one in the car hesitating, no one being the voice of reason suggesting we slow down. We were all in it, ready to race the wind. He cranked it to 120 … 125 … 130 … the huge engine roared, and we all laughed out of the windows into the summer air.

Brown-haired-boy slowed and turned onto an unknown country side road, which at the time I thought was in the middle of nowhere (Acuff Road). I now realize we were not that far from one of the high schools. He rumbled to a stop and said he had to let the engine rest. He shut off the car, with the engine ticking as it cooled. He reached for me to come close. I was still green in this way, and I was drunk, but I was scared and sobering up fast. There we were, out in the middle of nowhere (seemingly) on a deserted country road.

He urged me closer and immediately came in for a feel and a kiss. I turned my head and waxed about the beautiful night and tried to catch a glance at Katy and the dude in the back seat. They were not getting close; her boy must not be as bold as the driver, I thought. I shrugged off my guy's arm and told him we better get going. He hesitated, smelling the liquor on my breath and probably thought I was going to be an easy target.

Country boy shifted and lazily reached for the key. He looked at me out of the corner of his eye, turning the key in the ignition, but the engine did not come to life.

"Ah," he said. "We must have overheated her. I guess we're stuck here." He wore a satisfying smirk and leaned back against the seat and started to reach for me again.

I looked at him sideways, then turned to face him full-on with an eye roll. "You actually think I believe that?" I huffed out my nose. "We did not drive that far, nor that hard to overheat this fine piece of machinery."

"Well, you watched me! She won't start. Let's just give it some more time. Come here, we have time." He pulled me closer a little more forcefully. He tilted his head down for a hard kiss.

I slipped away again with a turn towards the back seat. Katy and the other guy were silent and staring at us. The second boy was not playing along with the guy in the front seat. Katy opened her eyes wide, letting me know she knew we could be in trouble and had entered into a dangerous game.

I squared my shoulders and separated myself from the driver.

"Katy and I would hate to have to get out here and walk," I paused and stared in his oh-so-blue eyes, "but we certainly will if we have to." I did not flinch, I just looked at him as if to say, "Whatcha going to do now?"

I was not about to be raped and left on the side of the road. He certainly wasn't going to play me with the "car won't start" bit.

"Why don't you give it one more try?" I asked, still staring at him.

He gave me a firm look, pulled his arm back, realized he wasn't getting anything easy and wasn't ready to take things forcefully.

Freckle-face turned the ignition, for real this time, and the engine roared to life. He drove back even faster. Maybe he thought he was going to scare us by going that fast down the narrow twisting backroad, but speed never scared me, nor Katy. The isolated road with two grown boys several years our senior was enough to be afraid of, but fast cars didn't scare us.

Nothing happened that night, and we would have made it hard for them; they would not have taken us easily. Both Katy and I were overly confident and would fight our way out of something. That was part of our friendship; if I punched her on the arm, she would punch me right back. We ran foot races with each other, even when we were supposed to be cool middle schoolers, and it was not uncommon for us to get scratched up in a self-started wrestling match. We were high energy tomboys, who happened to also be boy crazy. The events of the night, though, sobered us up, and we realized how stupid we had been to get in that car.

For whatever reason, we were lucky that night, and the boys summarily dumped us back to the wall on the edge of campus where they had picked us up. We walked back home, to the pig roast gala and the partying adults. The drunken drugged-out men now seemed scarier in the uncontrolled alcohol haze. Their leers, stares, and comments carried new meaning. Katy and I huddled back to my room and snuggled on my mattress on the floor.

Mom never asked about the bottle from the sewing machine drawer. I don't think it was hers. Someone must have stashed it there for later consumption, and no one thought to ask the teenage girls about it.

JANIS JOPLIN HAIR

It's review time at work. I have done well this year, I know it. "We," not "I." We have done well this year. I am looking forward to the review and to hear what my raise is going to be.

Bill, my boss, calls me in and asks me to take a seat. He shifts in his seat and glances at the review paperwork on the desk. "Okay, let's get down to it. Hope, you have done some incredible things this year. It's hard to imagine where we would have been without you. You know that, right?"

"Sure, well, I mean I hope so," I nod. "I love doing the project work, making a difference and improving systems. I totally love seeing the metrics—so fun!"

"Yes, you have done well and there is some other feedback we need to go over too." Bill shifts again, glances out the window, then puts the papers down and looks me in the eye. "You know we have been talking about career plans and what you want to do, right?"

"Right." I nod and meet his eyes.

"Well, has anyone talked to you about your appearance?" Bill asks, not shy, not condescending, just curious and direct.

"Um, well, no, not specifically. My boss at Eli Lilly did give me a career book for women, and there was a chapter on dress and what colors women should wear," I stammer. "I did go out and get some new work clothes this year when you promoted me." I hesitate, looking at him to try to read his response. "You mean like that?"

"Yeah, a little, but the clothing is not the thing I want to talk about today. I wanted to talk about your hair."

I put my hand to the back of my head and feel my hair. "Yeah? What about it?" I ask. I tilt my head, keeping eye contact, and now place both hands in my hair. I feel its bigness, the unruly curls. I had not yet swooped it into a bun secured with a pen or pencil, which I typically do by mid-day. "I mean, I know it is kinda big."

"Yeah, well that's just it. It's not bad, I mean you have great hair," he utters. "But with this new role and the level of visibility you are receiving, you need to look more, um, professional." He pauses. "Are there ways to make it, your hair, look more controlled? Or styled?" Again, he is being straightforward, not judging; he simply is asking.

"Sure. I guess. Of course. I mean, hair can be styled. I just have not gotten into the habit and only do it for weddings or special events."

"Well, you should think about it. There is a level of professionalism we need, and the way you present yourself is important." He nods. "While you are at it, you should consider some makeup."

I had been part of the HBA, Healthcare Businesswomen's Association, and I had read a ton of business books by this point in my career. The books, unless written by and for women, do not talk about these truths. I'd heard the saying a billion times: "Dress for the job you want, not the job you have." I had not internalized the information enough to apply the same concept to hair and makeup, only to my clothes.

I was not upset by this exchange—surprised, but not upset. Bill had talked to me earlier in the year about getting new clothes after a recent promotion. I had done that, but probably still had more work to do there too. Clothes, hair, and makeup were never important in my upbringing.

My hair is in its natural state is unruly and frizzy. I don't have pretty waves or curls; I have wild Janis Joplin hair. It takes an hour to get it to a controlled state with a flat iron or curling iron. I would do this when corporate visitors or clients came to the facility, but it was not part of my everyday routine. This conversation was an important moment for me.

I do not enjoy doing my hair, primping, and putting on makeup. It seems to take too long and feels like a waste of time. I now had direct feedback that it was something I should be giving time and attention to, and I felt a bit unsettled. I didn't automatically agree. It was a decision I was going to have to think about.

My career was, and still is, important to me. I was a single mom then, with two daughters, who I supported. I was the sole provider for my household. The success and salary I received at work was our only source of income, and I took that responsibility seriously.

I took my time with the hair decision. There were variables to consider. Who did I want to be? How did I want to define myself? Did I want to be someone who had perfect hair and makeup every day?

It may seem trivial, but it was not to me; somehow it seemed like a big decision to make. If I chose to do my hair and makeup every day, would that be like giving up on who I thought I was? Was I turning away from my upbringing? Mom had rarely worn makeup, and I'm not sure I ever saw her do her hair.

Appearance is an important question for all people, males and females, in the work place. Not specifically hair and makeup, but certainly how you want to be perceived and how you want to present yourself.

I had already achieved a certain measure of success of which I could be proud. *Did I want to continue to grow and succeed at work? Did that mean I had to do my hair every day? Was my identity of unruly hair and hippie upbringing who I was? Would I be okay just being a manager at a pharmaceutical firm and staying at the same salary? Do I stick with this life as it is?*

It took me two weeks to make the decision.

I talked to my mom, and she did what she always does. She was loving and supportive and talked about the pros and cons of each option, then said it was up to me. She reassured me that I would not be giving up on my identity, that I would just be doing my hair.

At the time, I had no female mentors at work. But

I had no qualms about it. Bill wanted me to do well, and he was wise enough to know that how I looked was a contributing factor to success. He also had the courage to talk to me. He did not find a woman or an HR person; he did it himself. He and I had developed an honest relationship where I could give and take feedback in an open and direct way. I am thankful we had the conversation.

My decision? I chose to start doing my hair and makeup. As I have grown in my career, I realize it is more about adjusting to the culture of the organization you are within. It has become my new norm. Now I feel out of control and messy if my hair is not straight. Of course, it is impossible to know how this decision affected my career. I may have been just as successful without doing my hair and makeup every day, but I doubt it. I didn't compromise my personal identity, and I didn't do anything that went against my morals. I now teach career planning, and I share this story. Who knows, maybe the next time I teach a career planning class, I will show up with my wild Janis Joplin hair!

LAKESIDE

Mom and her boyfriend Jacob didn't last. There was some kind of violent exchange between them. I don't know what happened, I wasn't home, I was at my dad's when she made Jacob move out. The story involved drugs and alcohol. Mom escaped and went to the hospital for stitches around her eye, and Jacob was now part of our history.

With him gone, the cycle of men through the house resumed. Waking up to loud drunken sex and Mom's late-night fun became the norm yet again. At least when I woke up to her and Jacob having sex, I knew who it was and who was in the house. The strangers brought with them the stink of danger.

Yet, in so many ways, I was still so naïve. Like my mother and my sister, I was comfortable and free with my body and clothing. I wore mid-drift shirts and tight shorts. That was just how we dressed. I thought nothing.

I was five-foot-seven, and my measurements were 36-24-36. I only know this because I am a rabid quantifier. I like to count and control. Numbers are safe, they are stable, they are predictable. I measured anything that could be measured, and I still do. I counted my clothes, which were color coordinated, and at any time I could tell you how many cans of soup we had in the cupboard. Numbers were safe, but our house wasn't.

I was lean, but curvy. I was tan and young. I had learned from my mom that my body was beautiful. I carried a bit of her come-hither swagger early but without awareness. Now there were too many men around. These men were "family friends" and were sent to pick me up from practices, from school, or from friends' houses. They took me to the store to get supplies for the house. It was always non-eventful until, one day, a family friend named Tim picked me up from Katy's house.

Unsuspecting, I scooted into the cab of Tim's dingy pick-up. He asked if I wanted to take a drive out to the lake. Nowhere I had to be, I said, "Sure, let's go."

The road to the lake was beautiful, tree-lined, and

twisty. It was better than going home to the messy house, with the haze of pot and drunken conversations as the adults played euchre for hours. Tim's beat-up truck took us through the rolling hills, the camper shell squeaking against the metal of the truck bed. We enjoyed friendly conversation as we made our way. I recognized the roads and fear never entered my mind. I was safe and comfortable.

It was late afternoon when he'd picked me up at Katy's house, and by the time we made it out to the lake, it was almost sunset. He stopped at a convenience store and picked up sodas and snacks. He suggested we sit on the tailgate and watch the sun dip below the horizon. I agreed, still not thinking beyond enjoying the snacks, fresh air, and beauty before me. The Be Here Now mantra can get you into trouble if your intuition is not developed.

As we sat facing the water, he comfortably draped his arm over my shoulders. I only then realized it felt like a date, or what a date might feel like. I was twelve, about to turn thirteen. He was thirty-four? Thirty-five? Why would a grown man want to spend time with me at the lake to watch the sunset? I did not tense up though. I remained relaxed. Yet I knew we were forty minutes from town, and I was not familiar with this side of the lake. There were no cars in sight, nor any passing on the road we used to get here. I was alone with a full-chested man, in the middle of nowhere.

Tim remained friendly. We chatted idly, ate our snacks, and watched the beautiful sunset. Immediately after the sun disappeared, the air got chilly. The blue-grey dusk held onto the light from the sun as long as possible, but darkness quickly settled with the cooler air, and I was ready to leave.

I crumpled up my empty bag of chips and wiped the crumbs from my hands in a movement of finality and turned to him. "That was beautiful. Ready to go?" I asked looking up with my face as blank as possible.

"So fast? There is a lot more to see."

"Really? What else do you want to see?" I asked. I was still young and did not realize that I could have replied, "Yes! I am ready to go." And maybe the story would have ended differently, but I walked through the door he opened and then shoved me through.

He leaned in and murmured, "There is so much I can show you." His hands were firm and unrelenting as he pulled me to him. The grip was not so tight to make me terrified, but strong enough to know that if I struggled the grip would only grow tighter. I was held fast. He yanked me up right next to him and gave me a forceful kiss.

He pried open my mouth with his probing tongue and moved his hand to cup my young breasts. I stayed on the edges, holding myself back, not leaning in, but not struggling away. I was scared. I knew there was nowhere to go, nowhere to run, and no one to yell for. My mind darted for solutions as the groping proceeded. He stopped kissing my unresponsive mouth and had moved to my neck. I knew I could not outrun him. I could not overpower him. I glanced around for options; there were none that gave me a way out. Up until now, he was acting like this was mutual. He was forceful, but not overpowering, using his thirty-plus years of adult experience to manipulate a child.

"I don't want to have sex with you," I said flat out. I was guessing that my best bet was to clearly state my position.

"Oh baby, how do you know?" He crooned and threatened, never ceasing the kissing, groping and feeling. Tim's hand slid up my shirt and under my small cotton bra. I remained rigid, unyielding. As he pressed up against me, I could feel his hard penis against my tummy. He stepped back and looked at me.

"Do you trust me?" he manipulated. "I won't hurt you, and if you don't want to have sex that's okay."

A little relief settled in. It sounded as if he would not rape me. He was still trying to play along with the date, pretending that hanging out with a young girl was the most normal thing in the world.

"I am still a virgin," I blurted out, fighting back my tears.

"And I don't want to take that away from you." His softened tone suddenly made me more afraid. "I won't hurt you. I just want to make you feel good and show you a few things."

He scooted me back into the bed of the truck and started kissing my neck again. He took my hand and put it on his penis, moving my hand up and down. I started to shake. With murmurs and whispers that everything was going to be okay, he got up on his knees and scooched his shorts down.

I sat outside myself, my thoughts blank and the black spot of fainting started to form in my mind's eye. Wanting to scream, feeling like I was going to throw up, I was also drifting away. I wonder if I had fainted what would have happened. Tim lifted me up to sitting, and he laid himself down. He bent me over his member with my face hovered over his full-upright penis and mass of black hair. He pushed my mouth down onto him. I gagged with each push into the back of my throat. His penis filled my mouth. With each thrust I could feel it grow.

Urging sounds slipped from his mouth and terror grew in my mind. I could tell an explosion was coming. Although his hand was still firm on the back of my head, I forced myself upward and sat back. Gulping air, shaking, I started to ramble. "I can't. I'm sorry. I can't."

He looked pained. I had clearly stopped a few seconds too soon. His face was pulled in a taut grimace and his hand hovered where my head had been.

"Oh baby, you got to finish. I am so close. You can tell that, can't you?" He started to plea.

"I can't. I just can't." Fear started to mix in with "rational" conclusions. *If he would just cum in my mouth, then I would not be raped. Maybe I should just do it?* "I'm sorry. I'm scared."

He put my hand on his throbbing penis. It was slick and ropey with bulging veins. I moved my hand, like he had before, hoping that maybe this would suffice.

The stiffness started to slacken, and the grimace did not pass from his face. I had stopped before the explosion, which was now backed up somewhere pressing his need to finish and my hand would not do, because I did not know what I was doing.

"I won't hurt you baby, I promise. Just let me finish." He whispered between gritted teeth. He helped me move my hand on him. He pulled my disheveled shirt by the shoulder trying to pull my face to him again. But I pushed back. "I can't! I'm sorry!" I was shaking and tears spilled from my eyes.

Maybe it was my tears. Maybe it was the firmness of which I spoke. Maybe it was because I looked sick. But he did not force me to do anything and relaxed his grip. I crawled out of the back of the truck. I straightened my shirt and bra, thankful that my shorts were still on.

I walked in the clearing. I breathed in the cool night air, tried to clear my head, and held my vomit and tears at bay. Maybe he could finish himself. I had no idea if that was possible, or what he was doing, but I was not in the back of the truck with him. There was that.

I didn't know how I was going to get home when he yelled, "Let's go," and started the truck. I got back in the cab and sat as close to the door as possible. No words were spoken on the drive home or ever again between us.

After that night, I did a better job of steering clear of Mom's brood of men who hung around the house. I no longer gave hugs and never again did I take a ride from the "family friends."

KFC

Despite her less-than-stellar parenting skills, Mom always held down a job and taught me a good work ethic. My first job was at age twelve. During the summer, I rode the city bus or walked to the locally owned free newspaper office and wrote ZIP+4 address labels for two dollars an hour. Katy and I also worked for her parents. They owned rental properties, and we did the turnover cleanup in between tenants. We cleaned the houses, painted, re-wallpapered and shampooed carpets.

I worked every summer for the newspaper and Katy's parents until I turned fifteen and got my worker's permit and a "real" job. Katy and I both got hired at the Kentucky Fried Chicken right next to our school. That same summer Katy and I painted and cleaned the carpets at one of her parent's rental properties, and we cooked up a plan to move into the place ourselves as the next tenants. We were both working, so we could pay rent and utilities. Neither one of us had our driver's license yet, but we figured that wasn't necessary; we walked everywhere, and this house location was centrally located. We could walk to school and to work, an easy two miles.

We made a formal presentation to her parents. We wrote up a proposal and made a PowerPoint slide deck, which at the time was in its infancy (little did I know how many slide decks I would make in my lifetime). The proposition included how much rent we would pay, that we would put the utilities in our name, and that we would pay for our own food and household supplies.

Such pomp and circumstance were not necessary for my mom. Lori had moved out when she was sixteen. I was soon to be sixteen, and I simply mentioned the idea in a casual conversation with Mom, who was in the throes of yet another period of heavy alcohol and drug use. She was too doped up to care, or something inside her knew this would be good for me. Her only stipulation on me moving out was that my grades could not slip. I was 27th in my class of 375 students with a

3.8 grade point average. I agreed and moved out on my own at age fifteen.

Katy and I lived together, worked together, and even shared a locker at school. We walked to school, then to KFC, worked until close, then walked the two miles to our home. We got checkbooks and state IDs so we could cash checks. We walked to get groceries. And we walked the railroad tracks.

The tracks were our special place. Much like their original design and purpose, those tracks were our lifeline. Katy and I walked home from work on the tracks, to and from the grocery store, to the empty warehouse, and to Clenchfield, a place made only in our minds.

Clenchfield became a place, a real place, that could be anywhere where the sun shines bright and the summer breeze was soft and warm around your whole being. Clenchfield was the place of childhood dreams and happiness. Long grass waved lazily, blue skies dazzled, and puffy white clouds dotted the sky. We discovered (well, created) Clenchfield as we sat atop a parked train car one happy afternoon.

The train yard was half a mile south of our house, and train cars, some filled with supplies and some empty, sat linked together in seemingly random ways.

Many summer afternoons were spent crawling on top of, inside of, and all around the train cars and empty caboose cars. It was quiet there, and we liked it, our small-town train yard. In all the years we climbed around there, we only saw one worker. Who knew how the trains were managed, how they linked up, or switched around. We didn't care. We felt the magic in being there alone.

One afternoon we sat on top of a train car, letting the warm sun rest on our faces. The crickets and bugs chirped and buzzed the afternoon away. A few tracks away from us was a train car with the word CLENCHFIELD inscribed on it in large black letters.

"Clenchfield," Katy stated.

"Clenchfield. Where is that?" I replied.

"Somewhere in the South. It's a farming community."

"Yeah, they have a main street, a dime store, a Dairy Queen, and a gas station."

"And one flashing red light at the main intersection." We smiled as we meandered along the images coming to our shared mind.

"No community swimming pool, but they do have a big pond, that they call a lake, at the edge of town that the kids use in the afternoon."

"Yeah and the eighteen-years-olds sneak to at night to drink . . ."

"Everyone's last name is Clenchson, and they have to go to the neighboring towns to find dates."

"The bus ride to school takes an hour because they are so far away from the high school."

"No post office. The bank is in the next town over."

"But they have a train depot."

"It was built when they had a glass manufacturing plant. They made those glass things that go on electrical poles."

"Yup. But it is always warm there."

"Yes, it is always summer."

"Yes!" we agreed. "They do have thunderstorms, but never tornadoes, and the kids, and adults alike, dance in the warm rain."

"The breeze carries the scent of honeysuckle and mulberries."

"The afternoons stretch into evening, and the people of the town read books on their porches, while the kids catch fireflies in the front yard."

This town exists outside of space and time, but was real—to us. We felt it, we knew it, we have been there. We surmised we lived there in an alternate life and wondered if it is pre-Hope and Katy-historic. Katy and I created Clenchfield together there on that day, and in a parallel reality, Clenchfield exists. We spent the entire afternoon building this place, this town, these people into being. From that day on, we would go to Clenchfield together. That could mean on top of the train cars, or just a sunny, happy place when one of us was down. That is who we were, who Katy and I were together. We were one and the same.

We spent a lot of time together, and Katy and I claimed each other as soul mates. We worked together, had many classes together, shared a home, and slept in the same room. We competed in grades, in school, and who could run the fastest down the street—but lovingly, and were genuinely happy for the other's success. We dreamt the same dreams, and more than once I spoke to her in my sleep. I once asked her for a quarter, so she happily got up and got me one in the middle of the night.

We walked barefoot on the train tracks, and the chunky rocks toughened our skin. The hot metal of the iron tracks burned callouses on our feet as we balanced our way through our teen years, "holding on to sixteen" as John Mellencamp sang, as long as we could, even before we were sixteen.

We loved our small, sparse house. We had two twin mattresses on the floor in our front bedroom. Our closet was a mix of our clothes that we interchanged at will. A leftover queen bed was in the extra bedroom that Susan camped out in most weekends. Our girlfriend Jamaica moved in when she got out of school for the summer.

Jamaica rounded out the group. She had experienced a stint through the commune with Katy and I. Afterward, her mom joined an Ashram and moved them to Boston when she was nine. Jamaica was one year older than us, but she did not have her license yet either, and she was accustomed to walking everywhere too. Her father still lived in Bloomington and she came home for summers. Through our mothers' efforts, she and I stayed connected. I made trips to Boston and when she was in town we had play dates. Jamaica was critical to our fun for that first summer we were out of our parents' homes. She was reliable and wildly measured, never getting too excited or upset about anything. She was, and still is, the ultimate in cool. She stayed in the middle bedroom, which everyone had to walk through to get to the bathroom.

The living room had a huge round oak table, but no chairs, and mostly we sat on the floor. A large mirror rested against the wall where every morning we sat and brushed our hair. We had zero kitchen furniture. The dining room was empty, save a crazy yellow pill-shaped lamp that we had made and the list of house rules we had dutifully written on a piece of plastic sheeting. There was an old, beat-up washer and dryer and a tilted broken small pool table in the unfinished cinder block basement that we thought was pretty cool.

The lamp was a giant yellow cylindrical plastic thing, maybe two or three feet in diameter, that we had salvaged from the warehouse near the tracks. It reminded us of a Nuprin pill. It was hollow, and we cut out the bottom of it and put a lamp inside so it glowed. It was a bright, glowing yellow pill in the corner of the dining room. We thought it was the coolest thing ever.

The House Rules were written in black Sharpie marker on a yellow and white striped plastic piece that we also found at the warehouse. It looked like a striped beach towel, but was flat heavy plastic. We had three House Rules.

1. No shoes
2. Do your own dishes
3. ......

We could not think of a third rule for the house, so we left it blank.

We had Sharpies all over the house and eventually anyone who came over signed their autograph or made some sort of graffiti on giant Nuprin pill lamp and the plastic beach towel sheet. We also had other pieces of plastic up, and friends wrote all over that. We wrote funny quotes and had everyone sign our walls.

Only now, as I type this, I realize—I recreated the commune. This home was largely empty, with shared resources. Twin mattresses on the floor. Various people coming and going. Strange how we create the thing we thought we were getting away from. This house, however, had fewer drugs and no partner swapping, but was similar in format and design to the commune.

We paid rent on the first of the month from the money we saved from our KFC jobs. Our food staples were Jiffy blueberry muffin mix (thirty cents and only required water), cereal, and Lipton noodle mixes. We always had a half gallon of milk, and otherwise it was all water to drink. Some days we would splurge and get the fresh lemon chicken breast. We could, and did, eat anything from KFC at no cost, except the white chicken breast pieces, we had to pay for those, so we had plenty of buttermilk biscuits and the expired pudding parfaits.

We loved grocery shopping, even if we did not buy much food. It was not uncommon for us to be at the grocery in the middle of the night. The greatest people shop at night. The morbidly obese, drug addicts, drunks, and drag queens shop in the middle of the night. All the beautiful and interesting people shop in the night. The three of us, Katy, Jamaica, and I, were living on our own, and we felt this is where we belonged. Getting our groceries with the people of the night was exciting, and even the trip to the store was a trip along the path of freedom. We walked in the hushed quiet of the night with the blackness folding over us. The tracks gleamed against the stray street light. We chattered all the way there and giggled all the way home.

Katy and I both turned sixteen at the end of August. Jamaica was a year older than us and had to go back to Boston when school started. We had to return to school, fresh from a summer of freedom. We had created our own rules and our own boundaries, yet school was a lifeline throughout my childhood, and I easily slipped back into the structure and schedule provided there. We also were excited to take our driver's test.

In Indiana at the time, you had to wait one month and one day beyond your birthday to get your license. As we counted down the days, we pondered how to get a car. Katy's solution came easier than mine, as her parents gave her an old Honda Civic. I had to scrape and save for the money to get my car and managed to save $500. Mom hooked me up with one of her friends who sold old VW bugs and said I could get one in that price range. A Volkswagen Beetle. Of course. The hippie doesn't fall far from the tree.

Mom's friend, Nathan, lived on Rainbow Road. Actually, he named the "road" to his house, which was just his driveway, but he made a sign for it, and it looked official. Katy drove me out there. We turned onto Rainbow Road and saw five VW bugs dotting the yard near the sprawling, crooked house. Katy had to get to KFC for her afternoon shift, so she dropped me off and turned her tiny Honda around in the dirty ruts and rambled off.

Nathan opened the door to me, smiling and waving.

"Hey, Hope!" he greeted me. "Would you like something to drink? Water? Tea? How is your mom?" He asked as he grabbed a single glass from a random mismatched set on the nearly bare and very dusty shelf. He filled the cup with water from the sink and handed it to me with a drip running down the dust on the side of the glass.

"Um," I stammered. I had not talked to my mom much since I had moved out. I went to her house to steal toilet paper, but I really did not know how she was doing. What could I say? *She's lost to addiction? In an alcohol haze?*

"She is good, I think."

"Good, good. Well, I hear you are looking for your first car."

"Yes! I need a car, and Mom said you had a few VWs that are ready to go."

"Yeah, I'm sure you saw them when you drove in," he smiled. Nathan walked into the living area and flopped onto a sagging, tan couch. I followed behind and perched on a wooden high back chair across from him. He removed a pot tray from under the marred wood coffee table and began to sort and de-seed.

"Yeah," I eyed his movements. I leaned forward, elbows on knees and watched. "Which ones are ready? The light blue one? The orange one?"

Nathan kept to his work. He was quick, clearly practiced. He licked the edge of the paper and secured it down to the joint. "The orange one's not ready, but the light blue one is." A few more licks, and his joint was ready to go. "Do you think you want the blue one?" he asked as he flicked the lighter and held the flame against the end of the joint.

I suddenly felt very self-conscious. "Yeah, blue is my favorite color." I gulped another drink of water, fighting back my nervousness. What was I nervous about? I had watched people smoke pot my whole life.

Nathan inhaled deeply and held his breath, "Good," he coughed. "I like that one." He held out the joint to me. I looked at it. Should I smoke it? Is it some ritual? Like tea in the Middle East? Will we do this business deal over a joint?

I reached for the joint, holding it much less expertly, trying not to fumble it onto the floor. I held it up to my lips, like I had watched so many before, and inhaled. An easy inhale, taking in more air from around the joint than actual smoke. I dutifully held my breath and coughed. Hey, this was easy. I had seen so many people do it before, this was nothing. Then I coughed, my eyes watered, and I coughed some more. Still trying not to fumble the joint, I leaned forward and passed the joint back to him. He smiled knowingly, but continued.

He smoked. We smoked. I drank the whole glass of water. I got giggly and light headed. And then we negotiated the price of the car. Which was not much of a negotiation, because I only had $500, and I told him so. He started with $800; I told him I only had $500. He asked if I could come up with the other $300; I told him it might take a while and certainly not to-day. I went into my story. I was working forty hours a week, was a junior in high school, living on my own, and had rent and utilities to pay. He seemed to ponder my situation and, at some point, we settled on $500.

He grimaced. "Well, there are a few things we have to do before you can have the car," he leveled his eyes at me, serious.

"Um, okay," I half giggled back at him, unable to be serious with the pot high that was making me feel spacier and spacier. But yet I had a moment of panic as I felt the stares and unwanted actions of other men in the past. Nathan was staring at me, and I had no idea where this was going; I stopped giggling.

"I have to show you how to change the tires, the oil, and replace the fan belt before you take the car," he stated matter-of-factly.

I exhaled a sigh of relief. I was high as a kite, in balloon pants like MC Hammer, tube top and no bra, but we went out to the car, and I changed the tire, the fan belt, and he showed me how to do the oil. He repeated over and over that I would have to know how to do this as an owner of a 1972 VW Bug. We had at least two or three VW Bugs as I was growing up. I remember a dark green one the most. It was not uncommon for us to have to push start it. I can picture Mom riding in the front with the door open, Lori and I pushing from behind. Mom would pop the clutch, and the car would magically start. Just as I had recreated the commune, I was now buying a hippie car, just like Mom.

I gave Nathan my $500, and he signed the title over to me there on his rickety front porch. I clambered into my new car and drove down the muddy tracks towards home.

The car was an uncomfortable beast, but it always started. The seat coils threatened to poke through the ancient vinyl. I covered the thing in Day-Glo flowers, and glow-in-the-dark stickers dotted the ceiling inside the car. I secured and paid for my own car insurance, and got a new license plate from the DMV. I was convinced that I was the only person in my high school who had to buy their own car and pay for my own insurance. Even now, I suspect that was the truth. I felt very grown up, and I did not want for anything.

I had a capable body and mind, a well-paying job, and was doing well in school. Life was very good indeed. In fact, it felt like Clenchfield.

CONFERENCE ROOM

The large dark table consumes the room, beaten only by the oversized leather chairs that encircle it.[2] I am on time and I settle into my seat, to the right side of the head of the table. I've read enough business books to know where to sit.

A few folks are already there, seated, fiddling on their phones or pounding out a last email. Most of my colleagues are late, which is typical. We all rush from one meeting to the next, skating in five to ten minutes late for each one. It is rude.

The chairman enters the room, making small talk with the guy behind him. They laugh easily, in the confident but unreal way of the corporate board room. They are not really laughing, they do not really like

---

[2] This is not a specific event, but an amalgam of meeting experiences. This does not represent my current employer.

each other; everyone knows it about these two, but they do a good job of playing the part.

The chairman takes his seat at the head of the table, gives me a curt nod, and looks to the vice president of operations, "Are we ready to get started?" He knows that we start when he says.

"Of course." The vice president launches into the mumbling agenda for the day.

I sit back and my eyes roam the room, taking in the body language, position, and engagement of the attendees. Everyone is dressed well, not overly so, because you do not want to try too hard, but certainly I can't show up with Janis Joplin hair.

I lean back in the leather chair. I smooth my black skirt on my legs, which are growing wider as I age, no matter the effort I put into diet and exercise. I listen to the discussion and ponder for a second.

How did I get here? How do you go from commune to corner office?

The transition is a lifetime, and I still have a lot to learn. Although in my career I have yet to have a colleague with a similar upbringing, I do fit. I intellectually can do what these folks do. My eagerness for a challenge or problem to solve, followed by my persistence and focus, are the reasons I have ended up here.

I push past problems or barriers that foil the less hungry. Or find alternate solutions along the way to ensure the reality of my ultimate vision. I do not get too attached to one solution, but take new information, new data, as it comes and adjust as I go. Being comfortable with change, in this day and age, is an asset. Companies today are constantly evolving and transforming. My upbringing was a perfect proving ground for being comfortable with change.

I thrive in chaos. I crave creating order. This started in earnest at ten and started cleaning my room when the remainder of the house was in disarray, and now I apply those same skills at work.

That is how I got here. I fit. I can do this.

Ben, at the other end of the table, brings up one of our poorly performing vendors. He is starting to discuss our options of dealing with them.

It is my turn to contribute. There is a balance in these settings. I do not always speak, because prattling on does not denote intelligence, but this is the right time for my input.

I lean in and start with, "Gentlemen, here is what we should do …"

As I share my thoughts, I notice the eyes on me, some distracted but others nodding ever so slightly in agreement. Yes, I do belong here.

This felt right, same as smooth pavement below my feet, running with a lean thirteen-year-old body; my words flowed easily and I knew my guidance was sound.

RAZED

As summer was coming to an end, Katy and I decided to go to the warehouse. We had discovered it one day earlier in the summer when we first moved into our house. It was just north of the railroad tracks, and we had wondered what was in it. We'd never seen any cars around there or any evidence that folks were coming and going. So, true to form, we found a way in.

The lights in the warehouse did not work, or we never found the right switches, so some of the dark spaces and the basement were never fully explored, but we rummaged through every corner we could of the areas that had light from the windows. The building apparently was used for storage of big yard items, decorations, and signage. The giant Nuprin pill was discovered there, as was the yellow and white plastic sheeting. We once carried home a row of auditorium chairs. Three metal auditorium chairs with red burlap seat covering, still connected to each other, was the prize of that day. However, when we put them in the living room, they kept falling forward because of the angle of the footing. We finally leaned them against the wall, but they never got used because of the forward lean. Fun to look at it, not useful. We then became more discerning before we decided to lug home items. Giant snowmen, big signs, and other random stuff were found among all the interesting junk there in our visits throughout the year.

We felt like brave explorers and knew a trip to this treasure chest was warranted before we called an end to summer. It was early in the morning, and the faint light of the sun was peering over the horizon as we made our way down the tracks. We took turns balancing on our own track, seeing who could walk along its narrow edge the longest without falling off. We were quietly discussing the things in our lives. The almost-whispered words respected the dawn and the coming of a new day, with the quiet that settles on the world at this time.

The bugs were silent, the dew was heavy, and the day was not yet born. The bushes and weeds grew close around the tracks, crowding our way and occasionally brushing our shoulders, leaving behind the wetness of the night air that had settled on the green fronds. The purple bunches of clover blooms and honeysuckle breezed by our noses, and we appreciated the time together on this hushed morning.

As we neared the warehouse, the bushes opened up to give way to the parking lot and the alley that ran on the other side of the tracks. The sun broached the line, taking a firmer hold on the morning. We started to disembark the tracks and head over to the warehouse and, as we looked up, we stopped in shock.

It wasn't there.

The warehouse was gone. All evidence of the building was void too. There was no pit or pile of debris from a recent razing. We stood and stared at the parking lot with only flat orderly dirt where the warehouse once had been.

It was like a dream, in the just-dawn light, an alternate reality where the warehouse had never existed. Had the building ever really been there? We had proof, insomuch as we had items we had snuck out of there. Other than that, there was no evidence of the building or the items it held ever really being there. Were our lives like that? All of life? What was the purpose we were holding? Were we forgotten items in a stray warehouse? Could we so easily be razed from existence with nary a mark left behind?

The dumbfounded look on my face could only be beat by the one on Katy's face. We stood there, staring, wide-open mouths, foreheads scrunched in attempt to understand. We looked at each other and burst into laughter. It was like that; we commonly laughed off our confusion and pain. And as much time as we had spent in the warehouse that summer, it was quickly gone, just as summer itself, and we were forced to move onto the next adventure or exploration.

School proved an easy transition for me. I loved an intellectual challenge, and my classes provided those opportunities. Katy and I took a college-level chemistry class, Susan joined too, so she could say she had one class with us. I was also loaded up with trigonometry, AP Spanish, government, and honors English. I do not remember spending much time studying, balancing work, home, and school, but I must have studied enough, as my grades stayed true and I was invited to join the National Honor Society.

Things got trickier the longer the school year went

on, but having to work after school kept us out of too much trouble because our day was full. Most days we would leave the house by 7:30 a.m. and not get home from work until 10:00 p.m. Many nights we would stay up late and only capture a few hours of sleep before the next day started. Eventually Katy dropped out of the chemistry class, and I was holding on for dear life to my Spanish grade.

My Spanish class only had seven students in it, all female, with a quirky non-native Spanish teacher leading the way. My Spanish final was looming, and I was ill prepared. I had planned to spend the week, and the night before, cramming as much Spanish into my brain as possible before the test. But the night before my final, a group of us from KFC decided to slip out to the quarries for a night swim after work.

Five of us piled into Katy's tiny Honda Civic. Getting to the quarries was always an adventure, as you had to avoid parking where any police might see you or where you might disturb any houses. A trek through the forest was always part of the game. We giggled our way from a secret parking spot and hiked the trails with a thin flashlight to make it to the swimmin' hole. Laughter filtered through the dark night air to us as we neared the site. Another group of party-goers had the same idea, and we made quick friends with the group of teenagers already there. Swimming in the black water, with the mystery of the universe alight above you, was always thrilling.

We stayed out late and, by the time we got home to our mattresses on the floor, there was only an hour before our alarm sounded for school. I don't recall if Katy arose and went to school with me, but I knew I had the Spanish final to face. Throughout the test, my eyes closed and my head fell to the desktop more than once. I got a D, the lowest grade I had ever received on a test.

My teacher was disappointed and called me in for an afterschool discussion.

"Hope," she started. "This is not like you. I honestly could not believe it when I graded this test." She held out the paper with the red letter D on it, shaking it slightly under my nose.

"I know," I whimpered. "I had to work the night before, and I did not get enough time to study."

She tilted her head, tssked and raised her eyebrows, encouraging me to expand. Clearly, she was not buying my story of work, which was true; I just left out the "staying out all night swimming in a quarry" part.

"It won't happen again!" I blurted out.

"Hmmm," she paused, seeing if I would take the bait and fill in the silence. I just stared at her with gentle pleading eyes, trying hard not to look at the paper in her hand.

She gave up, realizing I would not expand my story. "All right, then. See that it doesn't." She tssked again.

My shaking hand grabbed for the paper, and I welled up with tears as I swallowed my pride and snuck out of the classroom.

The teachers did not know we lived alone, or at least we thought that the teachers did not know. I know now that parents, teachers, coaches, and adults know way more about kids than is let on. The teachers know what many kids' homes lives are like. They take that knowledge and put it in their back pocket of information, and most use it to help motivate and encourage kids in the right way. This Spanish teacher was like that. I thought she was dorky, but she cared for the kids and wanted to see us do well.

She announced to the class two weeks later that, due to this being an honors-level class and unscaled grading, she would drop our lowest letter grade of the semester when compiling our final grades. This had to be a gift to me. I knew the other girls in the class had done well on that last test, we were honors students, and all we did was compete for good grades. But I also knew that all the students would benefit from having the lowest grade of their semester dropped. It was a great solution as a teacher; if you were a bad student, then you would have more than one bad grade, but if it was just a bad day, a bad test, or if you stayed out all night the night before to swim with strangers, then you were given another chance.

I am grateful for this and all the many times in my life I have been given another chance.

I am one, or maybe three, bad decisions from being dead in a ditch; but somehow I made it through.

ENTRANCE EXAMS

It was a picture-perfect day. Hot, but not ridiculously so for southern Indiana in August, with an intense blue sky, the occasional white stratus cloud, and the crisp green of the trees reflecting against the bright heavens. Well, the day felt like heaven to me.

I walked across campus with purpose and intention and an air of confidence and expectation. Trekking across the storied beauty of the university grounds, soaking up the sun and fresh air, I made my way to the building where our entrance exams were to be taken. I had already spent a good portion of my life exploring these paths, so it was a familiar journey, but today was different. I was on the edge of becoming. Becoming what, I wasn't sure. An adult? A student, I guess.

When I arrived at the registration desk, I felt the light sheen of sweat on my body and warm glow of my mind invigorated by the two-mile walk from my house. I signed in and got my packet of material with the agenda for the day. Orientation was at the cafeteria, and I was surprised to see how packed it was. The bench seating was loaded with parents and kids preparing for their day as newly minted college freshmen. I sat down and glanced around. I felt ready to go in my serviceable shorts, light T-shirt, and my wild mass of hair pulled back in a ponytail.

The welcome session kicked off with a lively crew of juniors and seniors offering a few quips and jokes, providing a brief history of the university, and giving a general map overview of the campus. Then things began to get serious. Our hosts talked sternly to the parents present, reminding them that they and their children would be separated. The students would take the testing sessions and then sit down with a counselor to select their classes based off exam results and their proposed major. It was repeated that the parents could NOT attend the testing sessions. The parents could NOT attend the session with the counselor. The parents could NOT attend the registration of classes. The parents around me seemed distressed by this. Parents were going to take a walking tour through the arboretum, get a group parent lunch, and then be reunited with their children.

As these instructions were delivered, the parents grew increasingly anxious. Would they at least be able to see their child's test results? Would they be able to see and discuss the class options with their child before registration? Would they meet the child's counselor? Could they attend just as a silent observer?

As the parental anxiety and questions grew, I too started to grow a bit anxious. I looked around and only then realized that I was the only person (the only child) in that jam-packed room that did not have a parent present. I was seventeen years old. I had graduated from high school, I knew my way around campus, and I had lived on my own since fifteen. It simply had never dawned on me to bring my mother.

I lived in a rented house with roommates, my mom and I spoke routinely, she was involved in my life, but I just did not ask her to come. The parents' nervousness became my own, and suddenly my soaring confidence plummeted and I felt alone. The separation process began. We, the students, were to be moved to another cafeteria-like room to start taking the placement exams. In transition from one cafeteria to the next, I snuck off in the movement of people and found a pay phone. I called my mom. Luckily, surprisingly, she answered.

"Mom?"

"Hope? Whatcha need, honey?"

"What are you doing today?"

"Not much, I don't have to work until five, so I was getting some chores done. Wait, aren't you supposed to be taking your entrance exams today?"

"Yeah. I'm here. I'm all checked in." I paused. "That's why I called. Mom, I am the only one here without their parents."

"Really?" I could hear the curiosity in her voice.

"Yeah. I didn't think to ask you, and now I'm feeling like maybe you should be here?" I wondered out loud. "I mean, I read the agenda, the parents are not going to be with the kids most of the day. The parents are doing a lunch then a walk through the arboretum. Do you want to do that?" I questioned, but even as I spoke, I knew this made no sense. "There is a group dinner later tonight too, but I'm skipping that anyway."

Pause.

"Do you want me to come?" Mom asked. Simple and straightforward, like always.

"I don't know. I mean, not really. I guess. It doesn't

seem like it's worth it now. There was not much in the welcome meeting that was all that valuable." I hesitated. "I mean, I guess it seems sorta stupid, but I didn't know everyone was going to bring their parents."

"Well, I will come if you want; I can probably make it over there in twenty minutes." Again, a simple statement, no pressure either way. There to support me if needed.

"Nah, I will be in the testing by then. I should be good to go," I said. "I'm sorry, I just didn't know."

"Are you sure? I'll come. I don't want you to feel alone." I could hear and feel Mom's love.

"No. I'm good. Hell, I have no idea why all these parents are here anyway, seems weird." I felt my anxiety lifting.

"Ok, well, call me when it's over and let me know how it goes. And if you change your mind, and want me to come, I can come over any time before work."

"Ok, thanks Mom. Love you."

"Love you too! Good luck, baby girl."

After I got off the phone, I felt better and my confidence returned. I returned to feeling more perplexed why all the parents were there in the first place. I was reassured that I could do this, and there was nothing for my mom to do anyway. *What were all these parents doing here? Maybe they had to travel from out of town, and it gave them something to do for the day?*

It did not dawn on me until I had my own kids that other parents are more involved and manage more aspects of their children's lives for them than I ever experienced. Feeling better, my spring back in my step, I absorbed back into the mass of people and made it to the room for my test sessions.

This is where I was most comfortable: taking tests, accepting a challenge. I was a little nervous, not debilitating though; it was the good kind of juice you get when an exciting problem to solve is coming your way. We sat at six-foot-long white and grey flecked bench tables. Four students sat at the end of each bench, to create separation in an attempt to prevent cheating. Three boys were seated at the table I was at. They apparently knew each other and kept up their nervous chatter.

The first was a foreign language exam, followed by the math placement exam. The questions were easy. Some of the math problems were hard only in the fact that I had not done fractions since third grade or whatever, but they all seemed pretty breezy. I was also taking the chemistry and biology placement exams, but they were not to be taken by all of the students present. I stayed seated after completing the math exam. It was timed, and I turned over my test early and waited for the time to expire. The boy across from me was struggling, clearly his experience taking this test was much different than mine.

He seemed so terribly young, blond hair, goofy countenance, and nervous energy. He glanced up at me and winced at the completion of my exam. He glanced down at his friends to see that they were finishing too. He looked around for the monitors who were working the room. No one seemed that close to us, and some of the students at other tables had started to talk amongst themselves, seemingly completed with the exam.

The boy whispered to his buddy, "Hey, can you help me?" They looked around furtively, slid closer together, and his two friends proceeded to give him the answers to most of the test. I just sat there, bemused. These were not exams to get into school, they were to place you in the right level for that subject. It was not a pass/fail thing, it was an assessment to get placed properly.

I kept thinking by cheating on the test, this guy was going to be put in the wrong class that would clearly be too difficult. Then again, I wondered at the knowledge of his friends, *were they really helping? Were they any smarter?*

But what struck me the most was my "fit." I did not fit. I did not fit with the opening session because I was the only one without a parent. I did not fit with the boys at the table because the test seemed easy for me. And I did not fit because the desire to cheat at anything escaped and baffled me.

I did not fit. This was not a new feeling, but I had hoped that entering college was going to be different. *Who was I? How did I get here? Did I need more parenting? Why do these kids need so much parenting?*

I didn't have long to be lost in my thoughts.

The jovial senior hosts came around and graded the tests. I got all but one of the answers right on the math exam. The cheater got about half of the questions right.

That placement day was a success. I tested out of a full two years of college-level math, the first full year of chemistry, and a full year of biology. That would save me time and money, money I did not have. I left there with clarity—that I remained unlike other people, that I stood alone in my quest to move forward as who I was and who I was going to be.

EPILOGUE

My daughter Lauren grabs my hand and asks me to come upstairs with her. At six years old, she does not necessarily need me to, but she enjoys having me help her get dressed in the morning. As I walk behind her, I reflect on this role as a parent.

Lauren is the youngest of my four daughters. I have been parenting for over twenty years, and only now as I walk up the stairs behind her does this thought become unequivocally clear to me: A partnership, an agreement, was made in the ether, that my soul, my being, will care for this other being.

Before she was born, we agreed that I would care for her physical, spiritual, and emotional growth in this lifetime. My four daughters and I made a pact before they were born that I would care for them and raise them to the best of my ability, and we entered an accord of that nature in that realm.

Although I had not thought of parenting in those specific terms before, as a partnership, my attempt has always been to be there. To be here. To fully love. To love unconditionally. I want to ensure that my children feel my presence, my love, my support and truth standing solidly by them throughout their lifetime. I am not sure how successful I am at that effort, but that has been my attempt and approach to parenting since my first daughter Ashlei was born in 1993. I will be here.

I am not sure all parents feel this way, but I believe we all try to do our best. My irregular childhood was provided by a mom who was doing her best. My life stories do not stitch together an orderly tapestry, but the love, the truth, and the being there come through.

In this moment where I walk behind Lauren on the stairs, I see my mom. I see my efforts as a mom mirror the efforts of my mom, Paula.

She was there. Mom loved us unconditionally, and we knew that. She worked and bought groceries when she could. She helped us get dressed when we were young. She was there with a chore list on Saturday mornings, and prepared our meals, washed our clothes and occasionally gave us baths.

She loved us. She loves us.

She taught us to believe in ourselves. We absolutely knew we could do anything with our lives. She taught us not to steal, cheat, or lie—these were unacceptable behaviors. We were told we were beautiful, strong, and intelligent. We were taught to be fully responsible for our actions and the consequences for our actions would be our own to bear.

In all the most important ways, she is a great mom. And somewhere in the ether, I agreed to enter into a partnership with her. We made a pact, and we both kept our end of the deal.

POSTSCRIPT

Lori's life is a wild success story, with unbelievable events that rival the Forest Gump storyline. However, her story is hers to tell. She is highly controlled and rarely angry these days. When she and I are together, we laugh, the awesome belly laugh that makes tears roll down your face and leave you giggling the rest of the day. I encourage her to get angry sometimes and be less controlled. She and mom have achieved a measure of peaceful late-in-life reconciliation.

My dear sweet Susan is wildly successful in another way. If there is a single marriage in this world that I have ultimate faith in, it is hers. She and her husband stand strong together. They are raising two beautiful girls and are working hard, much like her parents did before her. They live on a beautiful piece of property covered with lightening bugs and happiness. Susan loves and accepts all types of people, and she has shared that with her children. She is a rock, predictable and strong. She and I talk weekly, visit at least once a year, and I am so grateful she is part of my life.

Jennifer, my college roommate, who taught me how to live peacefully with people, is living happily in Southern Indiana. She has a menagerie of pets, a son, and a happy second marriage (second marriages are really the best, unless you have a first marriage like Susan's). She teaches elementary school, cooks frequently, and raises chickens. She, too, comes and visits annually for a candy-making tradition she shared with me. She is amazing, and I am thankful she is in my life.

Jamaica Rose is a critical part of my upbringing, having spanned my entire childhood, and she takes a starring role in my next book. She saved me, and Ashlei, from myself in my early twenties, and for that I am forever grateful.

In addition to these ladies, we had four other close friends in high school who were part of our "commune." The seven of us in our "group" spent all of our time together, some lived with us off and on, and we all experienced our first taste of freedom together. That included drugs and alcohol. Of those seven, four are dead or lost to addiction.

My precious Katy was my soul mate for a period of time, and her story is not mine to tell. We were supposed to move through that portion of our life together, in perfect resonance. We were partners, we were a pair, and I deeply, inexplicably, painfully love her.

Bill, Joy, and all of the folks who invested, fostered growth and learning in me, all the leaders, mentors and people in my life—both at work and in my personal life—are part of the reason for any success I have experienced. We cannot do it alone. We do not do it alone. Opportunity comes in strange ways, people must help, and I am deeply thankful and appreciative to all of those who helped me along the way.

And my mom? She is sober now. Mom maintains a positive outlook and believes good things are to come for her, her children, and grandchildren. Even throughout the addiction cycles, the happy smile remained plastered on her face. Although not in the best of health, she is an active part of our life. When I walk into her house, I feel at home. She feeds me. I can even take a nap, and she watches my daughters. I wouldn't be who I am without her and hopefully it comes through in these pages that I love and appreciate her deeply. She did her best. Her love is clear and strong. We share a bond forged in the ether before time.

POST POSTSCRIPT

As a young parent, my goal was to be exactly opposite of my mom. I was not going to be a waitress. I was not going to be an addict. I was always going to be with the father of my children. I pushed hard to escape the constraints of being poor. I pushed hard to be anything other than what my mother was—at least on the surface. Without realizing it, my core effort, my core approach to parenting, was hers, is hers. And is her gift to me.

In my attempt to not do the things my mom did, I stayed with the father of my first two children beyond a healthy point. Way too late did I realize that this man was damaging the growth and development of my daughters; and this was the final thread that drove me to divorce. He could do to me whatever he wanted, but once I realized the damage to my children, only then did I break my vow to stay with the father of my children for their lifetime. This was a promise I had made to myself while my mom was on her fourth marriage and my dad on his fifth. There is little in this book about my father, but he too loved me and showed me an unshakable foundation of faith and love in me as a human being. My story with him is for another day.

The way I grew up was unconventional, but there was no judgment, there was no categorization of others. I learned to accept people for who they were. There was no race, no color, no religion that was not accepted and readily welcomed. Same sex couples, mixed race couples, all were just people. There were no boundaries, no expectations, and no preconceived requirements.

These truths became part of me. This part of my lens to see the world remains. I simply do not categorize people per their ethnicity, race, or religion—or anything. I see each individual as human and become open to them in that way, and place little to no assumptions about who they are. I consistently assess people based on how they behave, how they perform at work, how they treat me, my family and my children, and if they are trustworthy. I simply fail to automatically categorize anyone in any other preconceived way.

This is among the gifts I received from my mother and my childhood.

We, the children of the commune, were left to learn and be drawn to our own path. As a child I read the Bible, *Be Here Now—Now Be Here*, Tao De Ching, *Zen and the Art of Motorcycle Maintenance*, and many other books. As an adult I have read the Bible, the Kabullah, *The Field*, learned about the Red Road and Native American spirituality, Islam, Sikhism, Chakras, The Tao de Ching (and the Tao of Pooh), *The Art of War, The LITTLE BOOK, Many Mansions, The Shack,* and the list goes on and on.

I have meditated and chanted for three days on the top of a mountain only eating Ayurvedic food for a week. I have prayed in the belly of the earth in a steam-stoked sweat lodge. I have sung in a Christian choir, clapped my hands in a praise session, and watched people speak in tongues. I have received light in a Sukyo Mahikari dojo. I have participated in Catholic, Episcopalian, Born Again, non-denominational, High Holy Spiritual, Sikh, Native American, and Jewish ceremonies. I have danced to the beat of the big drum, prayed to the gods of physics and chemistry, worn a hijab, and partnered with the morning light streaming through the clouds. I have meditated through New Year's Eve in a Kundalini fervor. I have been sprinkled for baptism at age twelve and submersed in baptism as an adult. My spiritual path is my own making, an amalgam of all these things and more. The underlying message in it all I learned as young child: No judgment. Just love.

In my upbringing everyone had a place and was accepted for who they are. It just was and remains how I think. It has been an unwitting blessing I have shared with people, helping people open their minds and find acceptance for other people.

ABOUT THE AUTHOR

Hope Mueller is an author, inspiring speaker, and a results-driven leader who enjoys heading organizations, improving system performance, and launching efficient programs. She is a busy executive, sits on multiple non-for-profit boards, and has launched a local scholarship fund. She is also the chairman and president of a charitable organization that helps children and their families during critical junctures of their lives.

Hope's passionate about promoting and developing leaders, youth STEM activities, and in-need community support and investment. Her early years were marked by her experiences within a hippie commune that shaped her approach and interaction with the world, and allows her to create order out of chaos.

She provides value through the construction, training and mentorship of highly productive teams. She is a change agent with excellent strategic vision, tactical execution, communication and organizational capabilities. Hope partners to motivate teams and colleagues with a positive approach, investing in people and exceeding company goals. She has the rare ability to turn vision into reality.

Hope has a number of technical publishing credits on a national level, is an international speaker and she authors business articles focusing on career development and positive managing up techniques. Hope's debut inspirational memoir is due out in October 2019.

Hope lives in northern Illinois, with her husband and actively parents her four daughters and grandson.

You may connect with Hope on these platforms:

Email: hope@hopey.net
Website: www.hopey.net
Facebook: HopeMuellerAuthor
Twitter: @hpmueller242
Instagram: hpmueller242
Goodreads: Hope Mueller

Please turn the page to enjoy a preview of
Hope Mueller's next book, *Counting Hope*.

INDY 500

I stand just inside the living room near the entry door from the garage. I stand with my sister, Lori, my six-year-old daughter, Ashlei, and my baby, Olivia, still in her car carrier. The bulky seat is heavy on my forearm. The diaper bag and my purse weigh down the other side of me. Ashlei presses play on the answering machine.

The beeeeeep sounds. Laughter and other raucous noises emanate into my orderly living room.

"Stop. Stop." It's Matt's voice, but he is not yet talking to us. "Wait. I'm leaving a message for my wife."

"Oooooh . . ." giggles a female voice. "Ssshmmmm."

"Hey, hon. It's me. I'm at the speedway." Matt pauses. I imagine him putting his fingers to his lips to shush his partner. "Everything is pretty quiet here. Um.

No accidents." I can hear him smiling. "I'll be here the next few nights."

Click.

Lori looks at me and I at her. I roll my eyes, take a deep breath, and start to unburden my load. Olivia gurgles, unaware of the disruption to the room or our lives.

Beeeeeeeeeep.

Another message fires off. Intimate groans, a rustling of body movements, and more giggles emit from the machine. Ashlei's face contorts in a confused twitch. I stand up straight, still with the diaper bag and purse on my left shoulder, and hurry to the machine to press delete.

I turn back to the baby carrier and wrangle the five-point seat belt loose and lift Olivia out, putting her to my chest.

Beeeeeeeeeep.

"Hon, hon," Matt's hiccupping joy continues. "I am at the racetrack, you know, for work. Um . . ." He is distracted by something, and now we hear keys jangling. "I won't be home tonight. Everything is OK . . . wait! Give me those!" The phone thuds and bounces on the floor, the recording device not missing a sound.

I take another deep breath, shifting Olivia to my hip to press delete before the scene continues.

"What was that, Mama?" Ashlei asks. "Is Daddy OK?"

Beeeeeeeeeep.

The sounds of a playful wrestling match fill the room, complete with laughter, body rolls, and keys being tossed around. "Hey, hey . . . give me those . . . don't . . . hey . . . I think I am calling my wife . . . wait, just wait . . ."

Delete.

Beeeeeeeeeep.

"Hey, hon," Matt starts again. "I just wanted to let you know—" A moaning orgasm is being gleefully pitched for my ears. All our ears.

Delete.

Beeeeeeeeeep.

I cannot pro-actively delete the messages. I have to let them start to play before I can hit the delete button. I stand next to the message machine and hit delete three more times.

The room is still. The air crisp with the emptiness of sound. I am stone. Lori is stunned, a frown pulling at the edges of her mouth. Ashlei looks confused with her right hand caught in mid-air with upward open palm. We are all paused in motion. Except Olivia, who shoves her hand in her mouth and grabs at my shirt.

I know right then. The moment is clear. My head is clear. I decide. The solid tone of the electronic bell and those beeps confirm the decision. I feel relief. Maybe a little sad, but the pressure is forgiven with my absolute certainty.

"Mom," Ashlei asks, "What was that girl doing? Who was that? Who is Daddy with?"

"Baby, I don't know. It sounds like they were playing around or something." I make excuses for him, something I had been doing far too long, but what else could I say? I close my arms around Olivia, pat her bottom, then hand her to Lori. I bend to finish unpacking from the morning trek.

We had been at church all morning for Olivia's dedication ceremony. I committed to raise my daughter in a Christian, albeit non-denominational, way. I had stood at the front of the 200+ person congregation, with the other couples who had babies born in the previous six months, making that pledge. Matt was supposed to be with me, sharing in that vow. But vows are meaningless to him. Matt, an EMT for the

Indianapolis Fire Department, had got called into work to cover the Indianapolis 500. He had a legitimate reason for missing this special occasion. It was not until I returned to my cushioned pew-seat and my neighbors asked me where Matt was, did I realize I was the only single person up there at the front of the church. Not single in the not-married sense, but single-without-the-other-parent-there sense.

I had stood alone holding Olivia, in my ugly floral skirt, pink shirt, and cream cardigan. It never occurred to me that it was odd I was up there without her father. I did not think to be embarrassed until several people asked about Matt. Only then did I start to be upset that he was not there.

I did not need him. I did not need him to stand with me and commit Olivia to anything. Only when my fellow church-goers noticed it did I grow angry that he wasn't there for Olivia. She is his daughter too; why shouldn't he be here? The frustration of his absence followed me out of the church and was nursed in my thoughts as we drove home and still coursed through me as we entered the house.

The tone of the answering machine popped the bubble and released me. This was the last straw in a series of thousand straws, whose pile gained height and weight on my still-young shoulders. It is done. It is decided.

A few days later when Matt comes home, I sit on the edge of our bed, with silent tears.

"I want a divorce."

I am not mad. I am not loud. I state it.

He laughs. He thinks I am playing. But my eyes tell him I am serious.

"Well, we can talk about this later. You can buck up right now. We've got plans tonight and we are not going to keep our friends waiting."

Matt traipses to the closet to switch out his work shirt. "Let's have fun tonight." He looks back at me on the edge of the bed, the tears dribbling off my chin. He comes over, touches my hair, and plants a quick kiss on the top of my head. "Let's have some fun. I will make it up to you."

I watch him and know he does not understand the depths of my commitment to the decision, but I will suck it up for the night. I wipe the tears with my palm and use the back of my fingers for the other cheek. Sniffing and blinking, I stand up to fix my hair and dab on some powder. No one would know I had been crying. No one ever knows.

We go out to dinner that night with another couple. Matt, of course, acts if nothing is wrong, because to him, nothing is. This is our life.

The four of us sit nestled together in a small booth, with Linda complaining about her husband, Rusty, all evening. As I pick at my Stromboli, Linda rants about how Rusty scratched the hubcap on her car. Rusty looks embarrassed and tired. He had taken her car to get washed as a nice surprise and the machine marred the hubcap. Linda was furious about it and will not let the matter drop. As she drinks her vodka and cranberry and laments her lot in life, all I can think is how she is ungrateful and stupid. She has no idea how good she has it. I never say a word about the answering machine messages, my husband's play time at the Indy 500, or how fucked my marriage is. I stab the sweet pickles on my plate and think I am done. I am done with all of this.

I am done.

ACKNOWLEDGMENTS

Wow. All authors and writers tell you this, but darn if it ain't true. A book is a massive group effort. There are so many people who have to make room, support and encourage the entirety of the process. The network is so wide and vast, I am worried about making sure I include everyone. My husband, Brad Mueller, was my first and most important partner in this endeavor.

My editing partner, Kelly Epperson, was critical to shaping this work into something readable (and enjoyable). Kelly was recommended to me by Dee Suberla. Brad, my husband, was the one who initially introduced me to Dee. Dee was an early supporter of my writing. As was my sister Lori and my girlfriends Meredith Merson and Melissa Alberts.

After getting the draft in working order, we submitted to six beta-readers; Jane Banning, Jennifer Hottell, Patty Klingbiel, Justin Robertson, Christian Brackett, and Michelle Parsons. Their feedback was deeply valued and some revisions, especially to the post-scripts occurred. Justin and Christian were both part of the commune and hopefully we will get to their stories in future works. Justin shared the different memories of the man who killed himself. I met Jane Banning at a writer's conference, attendance to which was recommended to me by my husband, Brad.

Jane Banning invited me to join an international writers and critique group, WAC, run by Joyce Finn. The inclusion and support from this group proved invaluable. The ability to have material critiqued and critique other's material routinely improves an author's writing exponentially. There are over twenty women around the globe who participate in this critique group and I thank them all. Their wisdom, honesty and writing chops shaped and improved my writing more than I can adequately describe, or likely even understand.

Patty was an early supporter and she brought in Jeremiah Worth for early marketing and publishing discussions. Jeremiah introduced me to a publisher and helped build the initial framework of my website. CG Life and Connell Group are both awesome companies and their early support encouraged me to proceed.

My publishing and marketing partners, Beth Lottig and Tiffany Harelick, are amazing, brilliant partners who are operational rockstars and use a bracing honesty that I do not get to experience often in my corporate life. These people were recommended to me from Jim Hohl, who was recommended to me by my husband (again).

As part of publication and launch we created a marketing team. The team is mostly made of people who know and love me and are interested in the success of this book. The team is Justin Robertson, Michelle Parsons, Carlee Parsons, Jody Haas, Jennifer Hottell, Jane Banning, Harry Jeffreys, Melanie Neal, Brad Mueller, Susan Chambers, Dan Larrimore, Katy Zabriskie, Sage Mueller, and Audra Coleman. Their input has been invaluable. Many people in this group were additional early readers of the book. Their feedback was exciting and served to sustain and buoy me throughout the past year. They were critical in cover design, back jacket copy, promotion, book signings and generating chatter amongst their network. The words I have written here seem insufficient to describe my appreciation for these people and their love and support for me.

I reached out to the company I work for to confirm this did not impact my real job. My firm has been hugely supportive. Kelly Jansen, Jason Riley, Holly Copeland, Chris Murphy, and Matt Flesh all knew about the work. They provided opinions and support, and their feedback came at critical points in my personal and professional life. Geoff Curtis, our chief communications officer, was quick to not only approve the work, but asked how else the firm could support me. Barry Moze and Mike DesJardin have been unequivocal supporters, without whom I could not successfully do my job or anything else for that matter. Shawaun Harvey, I owe you a debt of gratitude that I will never be able to fully repay. You have saved my bacon too many times to name. Thank you for your friendship and support in this lifetime.

People in the work must be thanked. I thank Anna, the only person I allowed to read her chapter before I used it. Her story is not mine to tell. Anna corrected some of my memories and approved the usage of her story. Since then we have reconnected and I feel blessed to know her and be a small part of her life.

I also thank Katy, Jamaica, Susan and Jennifer for their story is so intertwined with mine. Jennifer's patience is legendary. Her instruction powerful and I would not be the woman today without her friendship. Katy or Susan's have that same weight in my being.

Suz O'Donnell is my brand coach, another operational rockstar and also employs bracing honesty. She became part of the expanded marketing launch team. Suz provided critical feedback on bio generation, back jacket copy and of course the cover.

Helen Bloch is my attorney providing critical input and legal protection, especially when a last minute request came in for massive revisions to the print copy.

Already stated throughout the book, but it bears repeating. Thank you Mom for allowing me write this work and for your love and support. Thank you Lori for the sisterhood and early support for the book. Thank you Ashlei, Olivia, Brooke and Lauren for your partnership in this lifetime and letting me take time from you to do this work. Thank you Olivia for making the original design concepts of the book cover. Thank you to Tracey Morey whose support of this project and taking extra care of me and Lauren throughout the past two years (you are amazing) has been critical for my sanity.

This section would not be complete without the support of a team of folks who came out of the woodwork to help with the book. Kristie White-Scott, Jennifer Bushey, Jennifer Harp, Katie Dukes, Taylor Dukes, and Holly White were all a part of this effort. They joined forces with the previously mentioned marketing teams to make this book and launch a reality.

Brad Mueller. Even writing this acknowledgement section reveals how much of this work is yours and because of you. The introduction to Dee, the writer's conference, the marketing network, the support, the beta reading, the willingness to love and accept me in entirety, and the financial commitment to get this launched. There is more here than I can include appropriately, so I will leave you with 'You know how I feel'.

I could, and probably will, continue to revise and add this section and generate another 150 pages of thank yous. My gratitude to anyone and everyone who has supported and guided me cannot be adequately expressed.

There are literally not enough words to put on the page to all of the people who have connected during the last few months. Cousins, family, friends, and new friends have arrived. Our connection immediate and true. I thank you.

CPSIA information can be obtained
at www.ICGtesting.com
Printed in the USA
FFHW011931200919
55110363-60814FF